Higher Education and the Public Trust:
Improving Stature in Colleges and Universities

by Richard L. Alfred and Julie Weissman

ASHE-ERIC Higher Education Report No. 6, 1987

WITHDRAWN

Prepared by

Clearinghouse on Higher Education
The George Washington University

Published by

 *Association for the Study of*
Higher Education

Jonathan D. Fife,
Series Editor

WITHDRAWN

Cite as
Alfred, Richard L. and Julie Weissman. *Higher Education and the Public Trust: Improving Stature in Colleges and Universities*. ASHE-ERIC Higher Education Report No. 6. Washington, D.C.: Association for the Study of Higher Education, 1987.

Managing Editor: Christopher Rigaux
Manuscript Editor: Barbara M. Fishel/Editech

The ERIC Clearinghouse on Higher Education invites individuals to submit proposals for writing monographs for the Higher Education Report series. Proposals must include:
1. A detailed manuscript proposal of not more than five pages.
2. A chapter-by-chapter outline.
3. A 75-word summary to be used by several review committees for the initial screening and rating of each proposal.
4. A vita.
5. A writing sample.

Library of Congress Catalog Card Number 88-71516
ISSN 0884-0040
ISBN 0-913317-41-1

Cover design by Michael David Brown, Rockville, Maryland

ERIC **Clearinghouse on Higher Education**
School of Education and Human Development
The George Washington University
One Dupont Circle, Suite 630
Washington, D.C. 20036-1183

ASHE **Association for the Study of Higher Education**
Texas A&M University
Department of Educational Administration
Harrington Education Center
College Station, Texas 77843

This publication was prepared partially with funding from the Office of Educational Research and Improvement, U.S. Department of Education, under contract no. 400-86-0017. The opinions expressed in this report do not necessarily reflect the positions or policies of OERI or the Department.

EXECUTIVE SUMMARY

Colleges and universities are resource-acquiring institutions. They understand that positive public attitudes about higher education are important because they affect their financial stability and support of their academic programs. Faculty and administrators have come to recognize that public understanding and support for postsecondary education goals is important to institutional well-being. Given this reality, higher education institutions have no choice but to be cognizant of their stature with important constituencies if they expect to gain and hold public support. If colleges and universities are to enhance their stature in a period of rapid social, economic, demographic, and technological change, substantive strategies must be developed. Without specific action, most institutions will find themselves the target of continuing criticism by external publics, ranging from students and parents making decisions about enrollment to government agencies making decisions about financial appropriations.

The central topic of this report is not marketing, public relations, strategic planning, or management strategies to improve institutional visibility over the short run. It is rather institutional stature, its development and determination, and strategies for its enhancement. A constant theme dominates the report: Although colleges and universities are unquestionably affected by trends in the external environment, they can plan, respond, act, and organize themselves to improve stature. This report examines the deeper, more fundamental dimensions of stature and then moves beyond that examination to the dynamics of enhancement—the coordinated actions that institutions can take beyond marketing and public relations to address forces in the environment while simultaneously educating the public about important goals, purposes, outcomes, and benefits of postsecondary education.

What Is Stature?

Postsecondary institutions generally seek congruence between the social values associated with or implied by their activities and the values in the larger social environment of which they are a part. When an actual or potential disparity exists between institutional and societal values, a threat to stature will exist. These threats take the form of legal, economic, and social sanctions associated with changing attitudes and perceptions of the institution by external publics.

Stature can be understood as the aggregate of positive perceptions and representations held by specific individuals, groups, and publics in reference to particular characteristics and/or performance attributes projected by colleges and universities over time. Its forms of expression in colleges and universities are multiple, as are the contexts in which it can be viewed. Stature can be perceived in a macro context in which higher education exists as a sum of parts that together make up a social institution. It can be seen in a micro context in which individual institutions and campus locations become the units of analysis. Both of these contexts require consideration in the examination of stature, how it forms, and its consequences for colleges and universities.

What Are the Dimensions of Stature?
To comprehend fully the multiple dimensions of stature implicit in the preceding definition, it is important to array its dimensions in a model that will enable practitioners to understand features of the concept and the relationships that make each dimension relevant to the others. The model developed and presented in this report depicts stature as the product of (1) an *environment* comprised of multiple forces that influence the exchange of resources between colleges and universities and different constituencies, (2) *inputs* in the form of constituents' needs and expectations for educational programs and services that carry stimuli from the environment to the institution and induce decisions about programs and resources, (3) *attributes of organization and performance* that facilitate or retard institutional responsiveness to external constituencies by influencing important decisions related to domains of activity, (4) a *conversion process* that transforms constituents' needs and expectations and environmental stimuli into decisions about programs and resources, (5) *outputs* that carry the results of institutional programs and services to multiple constituencies in the environment, (6) *communication* that involves formal and informal procedures for disseminating information about outputs to constituencies, and (7) *feedback* that transmits public perceptions relative to the outputs produced by an institution in one period back to the conversion process as the inputs in a later period of time. Each dimension interacts with the others. Together they produce stature for an institution, or a set of institutions, in the form of constituents' perceptions of convergence among conditions, needs, and stimuli in the environment and the benefits

produced by institutions through educational programs and services.

What Are Organizations Doing to Enhance Stature?
In response to changing conditions in the economy, public opinion, and the behavior of competitors, profit and nonprofit organizations have instituted a variety of techniques to enhance stature. Measured through sales volume, corporate visibility, and change in public opinion, most techniques have focused on improvement in corporate products and services based on information about consumers' needs, preferences, values, and satisfaction. Significant resources have been spent on opinion research, marketing, improvement in services, and staff development to improve the public's perception of organizational products and operations.

Colleges and universities differ sharply from other complex organizations in certain characteristics. Institutions seeking to improve their understanding of stature and how it develops may benefit from the experience of other organizations, however. Business and industry, health care organizations, labor unions, and government agencies have focused efforts to enhance stature on assessment of elements in the external environment that are not easily controlled, such as social forces, public attitudes, and consumers' behavior. In colleges and universities, the focus has been on elements internal to the organization that can be more easily controlled, such as institutional publications, outreach activities, involvement in campus activities, and campus-based performance assessment. A few institutions have grasped the importance of institutional stature and, borrowing from successful practices in other complex organizations, have designed and implemented strategies to improve it. The majority of colleges and universities, however, have concentrated on short-term marketing practices that rely solely on communication activities.

What Can Colleges and Universities Do to Enhance Stature?
The dimensions of stature presented in the model, when examined in context with practices to enhance stature employed by different types of organizations, suggest four leveraging strategies that can become the focus of efforts to enhance stature in colleges and universities:

- *Strategic assessment*: Management of the effects of societal change on institutional programs, services, and resources through environmental scanning, monitoring, and strategic planning;
- *Allocation of resources*: Improvement of institutional responsiveness to changing external conditions through resource allocation systems that incorporate mechanisms for planning, feedback, and innovation;
- *Outcomes assessment*: Collection and publication of benefit-cost information describing institutional and student outcomes, expenditures, and costs as a means for demonstrating accountability to important constituencies;
- *Image management*: Management of public opinion through assessment of the effectiveness of institutional marketing and public relations techniques coupled with redesign of organizational communication strategies to create impact with constituencies.

The assumption underlying these leveraging strategies is that as institutions come to better understand how societal forces, public opinion, and organizational behavior interact to determine stature, they will move to develop activities that result in enhancement. Most institutions, prodded by recent criticism, have begun to develop marketing and public relations plans. Much energy is expended on these plans, with mixed results. An examination of what the literature has to say about complex organization practices and public affairs strategies employed by colleges and universities makes it clear that many of these efforts are cosmetic. They attack the symptoms of the problem, but they do not address the problem itself. Instead of piecemeal public relations efforts with selected constituencies, it would be wiser to develop a coordinated plan for enhancement involving the leveraging strategies presented. Instead of vesting too much faith in marketing and public relations plans that often do little more than temporarily appease certain constituencies, institutions can improve stature through altering their approach to management. The goal is this: develop assessment and communication systems that enable institutions to effectively anticipate and respond to external forces while simultaneously educating the public about important goals, purposes, outcomes, and benefits of postsecondary education. It is not sufficient, for the purposes of enhancing stature, to simply alter institutional programs and services based on information about the future. Stature will accrue to those institutions that convincingly demonstrate how they provide benefits to individuals, groups, and organizations that satisfy important needs and goals.

ADVISORY BOARD

Frederic Jacobs
Dean of the Faculties
American University

Hans H. Jenny
Executive Vice President
Chapman College

Joseph Katz
Director, New Jersey Master Faculty Program
Woodrow Wilson National Fellowship Foundation

George Keller
Senior Vice President
The Barton-Gillet Company

L. Lee Knefelkamp
Dean, School of Education
American University

David A. Kolb
Professor and Chairman
Department of Organizational Behavior
The Weatherhead School of Management
Case Western Reserve University

Judith B. McLaughlin
Research Associate on Education and Sociology
Harvard University

Theodore J. Marchese
Vice President
American Association for Higher Education

John D. Marshall
Assistant to the Executive Vice President and Provost
Georgia State University

Sheila A. Murdick
Director, National Program on Noncollegiate-Sponsored
  Instruction
New York State Board of Regents

Steven G. Olswang
Assistant Provost for Academic Affairs
University of Washington

Robert L. Payton
Scholar-in-Residence in Philanthropic Studies
University of Virginia

Thomas J. Quatroche
Professor and Chair, Educational Foundations Department
State University College at Buffalo

S. Andrew Schaffer
Vice President and General Counsel
New York University

Henry A. Spille
Director, Office on Educational Credits and Credentials
American Council on Education

CONTENTS

FOREWORD

Simply put, the "stature" of an institution is the esteem in which people hold it—its reputation. Clearly, an institution develops its reputation by what it does. The question is, does the public have an accurate perception of what comprises the institution?

Generally speaking, the concept of institutional stature is easily accepted. The concept of enhancing institutional stature, however, is often received with some suspicion. The suspicion derives from a concern over the motives and honesty behind a movement to purposely enhance an institution's stature. When we talk about public relations and enhancing stature, there is a philosophical and ethical conflict. Are we talking about putting on a new or a false face? Or are we talking about dispelling the haze so we can see the true face of the institution? Are the motives to present, more comprehensively and accurately, the public with a clearer image or face of the institution? Or are the motives more directed toward emphasizing only those aspects of an institution that are complimentary?

Obviously, a less than complete and truthful representation of an institution is antithesis to the principles for which higher education stands. It is an undeniable fact, however, that the American public and some elected officials often have an inaccurate perception about the image, reputation, and stature of higher education.

This perception has been seen time and time again, as exemplified in such books as Caroline Bird's *The Case Against College*. Therefore, like it or not, if institutions want to counteract these perceptions, they have a *responsibility* to see that the public receives sufficient information to form a more accurate understanding of modern colleges and universities. This can be done only if institutions have already carefully assessed the degree to which they are achieving the goals expected by the public and demanded by faculty, staff, trustees, students, and others intimately connected with its welfare.

In this report, Richard Alfred, professor, and Julie Weissman, research associate, both of the National Center for Research to Improve Postsecondary Teaching and Learning at the University of Michigan, develop a model on the dimensions of institutional stature. They have also identified specific activities that could be used by colleges and universities to evaluate specific areas that contribute to institutional stature, such as strategic assessment, allocation of resources, outcomes assessment, and image management.

Creating in the public an accurate perception of an institution is more than just public relations, more than mere image making. Stature assessment can be used to identify and improve internal weaknesses, and it also can be used to attract students with better institutional fit. The better the match, the lower the chance of attrition. Not only students but staff and faculty can benefit from stature assessment, particularly in the area of faculty recruitment. Understanding what goes into institutional stature, how it is formed, and how it is changed, is a skill well worth knowing. It perhaps can even save a school.

Jonathan D. Fife
Professor and Director
ERIC Clearinghouse on Higher Education
School of Education and Human Development
The George Washington University

ACKNOWLEDGMENTS

We are indebted to a number of individuals who made significant contributions in the development of this monograph. Mary Hummel, Louise Hessenflow, Gerlinda Melchiori, and Carolyn Kelley documented societal conditions and practices of complex organizations that are discussed in two sections of the report. Sandy Whitesell and Richard Bentley developed literature reviews to guide the analysis of complex organizations and practices to enhance stature in colleges and universities. We are grateful to Betty Piccione and Ardys Bloomer for their help in word processing.

Finally, we would like to acknowledge the assistance of Jonathan Fife and Christopher Rigaux of the ERIC Clearinghouse on Higher Education. Without their patience and support, this monograph would not have reached fruition.

INTRODUCTION

Faced with changing social and economic conditions, public policy, and public opinion toward higher education, colleges and universities are beginning to carefully examine their relationship to and the ways they deal with the general public. On the one hand, most recent surveys of public attitudes show a positive view of higher education. Although they question whether colleges render good value for the dollar, most Americans say that a college education is more important than ever (Yankelovich 1987).

On the other hand, colleges and universities are encountering major signs of discontent. Concerns about rapidly increasing tuition costs, scandals in college athletics, the quality of faculty and academic programs, the unfair use of tax-exempt status to operate money-making activities, employers' dissatisfaction with the knowledge and technical skills of graduates, intensified competition for students and resources, and poorly documented relationships between the costs and benefits of college attendance permeate the media. The issues have spurred harsh criticism in legislative chambers, on Capitol Hill, and in family discussions. Friends and critics alike have begun to liken colleges and universities to "big business" because of their increasing dependence on marketing and lobbying to acquire resources (Dill 1982; Pelletier and McNamara 1985; Trachtenburg 1984). Administrators and college lobbyists have been accused of behaving like the representatives of any other special interest. Secretary of Education William J. Bennett boldly pronounced that higher education's tendency to cry "wolf" so insistently and tiresomely "could eventually erode congressional support for colleges and universities" (*Chronicle of Higher Education* 15 October 1986).

Colleges and universities are resource-acquiring institutions. They understand that positive public attitudes about higher education are important because they affect college enrollment, financial stability, and support of academic programs. Faculty and administrators have come to recognize that public understanding and support for postsecondary education goals are important to an institution's well-being and that such support is necessary not only to offset the effects of economic and demographic downturns but also to provide a foundation for new programs and services that would align an institution with its changing external environment.

The stature of colleges and universities in the eyes of the public has become a prominent issue, and it is apt to remain so in the foreseeable future. Faculty, administrators, and governing boards find themselves accountable to a wide range of external agencies and groups that do not automatically ascribe value to higher education. Institutions and administrators, frequently to their distress, have discovered that the public perception of postsecondary education can change rapidly and that institutions are never secure in the eyes of the public. They have also discovered that preoccupation with critics and knee-jerk public relations strategies to deflect the harmful effects of criticism can result in the occlusion of fundamental questions regarding the stature of colleges and universities—questions involving an awareness of what colleges and universities do in a changing environment:

1. What is stature and how is it distinguished from concepts like image, reputation, marketing, and quality?
2. How does stature develop and what organizational characteristics contribute to positive or negative stature in colleges and universities?
3. What is the relationship between stature and prevailing societal conditions; do institutions experience growth or decline in stature as these conditions change?
4. What steps can colleges and universities take to sustain or enhance stature?

The literature on strategic planning and marketing in higher education supports the observation that colleges and universities spend too much time on quick fixes and short-term gains in admissions and fund raising and neglect the harder tasks that bring high stature—innovation, enhanced teaching, pursuit of quality, assessment of benefits and costs, for example (Hilpert and Alfred 1987; Keller 1983). This monograph brings into focus the larger issue of stature in American colleges and universities and requisites for its advancement in an environment comprised of trends, threats, opportunities, market preferences, changing consumer needs, and competition. The first major section provides a brief historical overview and working definition and attempts to distinguish stature from related concepts like image, reputation, and quality. The major heuristic device in the section is a conceptual model that identifies the spectrum of forces interacting to determine stature. The following section reviews major trends in public opinion toward higher education between 1965 and 1985—a period of major change in the fabric of American social institutions. Colleges and universities both influence and are influenced by public opinion. The objective of this section is to set the stage for a discussion in the third section of attributes of the academic organization that facilitate or impede the development of stature.

The fourth section reviews practices to enhance stature in public- and private-sector organizations outside of higher education, including business and industry, health care organizations and professional associations, government agencies, and labor unions. Many of the practices employed in these organizations have a direct application to colleges and universities and can be adapted for use at the institutional and subinstitutional levels. The section also identifies selected adaptations.

A summary section provides some conclusions about organizing colleges and universities to enhance stature that follow from the discussion in the preceding sections. The final section presents concrete suggestions for actions that faculty and administrators can take to enhance stature in a college or university.

The central topic of this report is not marketing or public relations or strategic planning or management strategies to improve institutional visibility over the short run. It is institutional stature, its development and determination, and strategies for its enhancement. A constant theme dominates the report: Although colleges and universities are unquestionably affected by trends in the external environment, they *can* plan, respond, act, and organize themselves to improve stature. Adopting short-term public relations and marketing strategies will not be sufficient to improve institutional stature. This report examines the deeper, more fundamental dimensions of stature and then moves beyond that examination to the dynamics of enhancement—to the coordinated actions that institutions can take beyond marketing and public relations to address forces in the environment while simultaneously educating the public about important goals, purposes, outcomes, and benefits of postsecondary education.

Stature in American institutions of higher education has been a perennial issue. With the advent of *Sputnik*, the public and its governmental representatives set lofty goals for postsecondary education. The goals for higher education were national—citizens made a commitment to technological and economic superiority over other nations. They were also personal—school-age youth and their parents believed that a college education guaranteed a prosperous future and style of life. The nation's postsecondary institutions attempted to build a system that would attain these goals (Mathews 1976).

Since the early 1960s, when these goals were set forth, many changes have occurred in the fabric of social institutions: the decline of superiority in world and domestic markets, economic recession, unemployment and underemployment of the educated, structural change in the family, advancing technology, political fragmentation, decentralization of government to the states, and privatization of human services. In the mid-1970s and early 1980s, societal prosperity declined, and the flow of public funds ebbed. Colleges and universities responded by instituting an array of cost-cutting and revenue-producing strategies aimed at maintaining the current scale of operations while simultaneously balancing revenues and expenditures. As the fixed costs of operation expanded and institutional efforts to improve productivity failed to compensate for declining resources, the attitude of governmental officials and others establishing policies for allocating resources changed to one of decreased confidence in higher education management coupled with a compulsion for greater control over postsecondary institutions. The federal government, private foundations, state legislatures and coordinating boards, and business and industrial organizations began to voice a need for information about the benefits of educational programs as a condition for investing more of their limited resources. It became apparent that if academic organizations failed to address effectively the relationship of institutional performance to social expectations, control over funding decisions would be farther removed from the campus (Folger 1980; Spitzberg 1980).

The attitude of governmental officials. . . changed to one of decreased confidence in higher education management.

Higher Education and Public Perception

Previous research has shown that individuals and groups usually express perceptions about colleges and universities through statements of satisfaction and dissatisfaction (Biggs et al. 1975; Brouillette and Rogers 1980; Moore et al. 1979; Owings 1977;

Smith 1983). Although research on institutional stature is sparse, what little exists points to the informal and subtle but definite channels of communication by which the images of colleges are transmitted. In the 1960s and 1970s, research showed that college selection occurred largely on the basis of hearsay and perceptions of quality (Grunde 1976). A panel study involving over 10,000 high school seniors demonstrated that students chose their colleges primarily on the basis of proximity, popularity, and perceived stature (Trent and Medsker 1968). Choice based on perception could be viewed only as irrational for consumers about to invest four years of time and many thousands of dollars in a college or university education.

In the mid-1970s and early 1980s, the concept of student choice as an index of institutional stature was supplemented by the concept of multiple publics engaged in "resource conversion" with postsecondary institutions (Davies and Melchiori 1982; Kotler and Fox 1985). These publics were classified into distinct behavioral categories—supporters, clients, consumers, internals, and externals—each bringing a distinct set of interests, perceptions, and values that interact to determine the stature of a college or university. Institutions improved or diminished in stature through perceptions held by multiple publics of the benefits they rendered and the relationship of these benefits to educational needs and expectations. Using this supposition as a frame of reference, it is possible to develop a working definition for stature and to identify some of its dimensions.

What Is Stature?

Postsecondary institutions generally seek congruence between the social values associated with or implied by their activities and the values in the larger social environment of which they are a part (Dowling and Pfeffer 1975). When an actual or potential disparity exists between institutional and societal values, stature is threatened. Threats to stature take the form of legal, economic, and social sanctions associated with external publics' changing attitudes and perceptions of the institution. The role played by individual attitudes and perceptions as a determinant of institutional stature is reinforced by the definition of an attitude as a relatively enduring but dynamic organization of beliefs about objects and situations (Rokeach 1968).

Combining the notions of "attitude" as an enduring and dynamic organization of beliefs about objects and situations and "value congruency" as a requisite for the development of positive attitudes toward organizations, institutional stature can be defined as *the aggregate of positive perceptions and representations held by specific individuals, groups, and publics in reference to particular characteristics and/or attributes of performance projected by colleges and universities over time*. This definition implies that the concept of stature can vary between a neutral and a positive connotation. On the one hand, stature is a matter of perceptions and representations held by the public. These perceptions could conceivably be positive or negative. On the other hand, stature can be viewed in the more common sense, as a positive attribute—something that an institution might want to elevate or enhance. In essence, stature encompasses both of these connotations. It is a positive attribute projected by an institution or a complex of institutions, and it is a function of perceptions that may themselves be positive, negative, or neutral.

This definition also implies that stature can be viewed in two distinct but interwoven contexts: (1) a *macro* context in which higher education exists as a sum of parts that together make up a social institution and (2) a *micro* context in which individual institutions and campus locations become the units of analysis. Although it is likely that stature develops through a process of association—the gains established by one institution or set of institutions becoming those of another—both of these contexts require consideration in the examination of stature, how it forms, and its consequences for colleges and universities.

Finally, the definition implies that stature encompasses a temporal dimension involving a delicate balance between continuity and change. Colleges and universities must simultaneously respond to and resist important forces of societal change if they expect to enhance or maintain stature. The stature of an institution is a product of both its historical legacy and its current performance. It differs from related concepts like "image," "reputation," "marketing," and "quality" in that it develops over time: It relates to a totality of perceptions held by multiple publics; it resists impulses to alter institutional domains of activity in response to rapidly emerging market forces; it is not easily transformed by a single positive or negative image-producing incident (a "snapshot"); it encompasses multiple institutional attributes, not simply those accounting for a single dimension of excellence or superiority; it may change over time in accord with circumstances in the environment; it can be cultivated with the public outside of a process or direct resource exchanges with the institution. As a concept, stature implies that individuals, groups, and publics acquire information over time, make judgments, and develop associations with a particular institution or complex of institutions.

Dimensions of Stature

To fully comprehend the multiple dimensions of stature implicit in the preceding definition, it is important to array its dimensions in a model that will enable practitioners to understand features of the concept and the relationships that make each dimension relevant to the others. The model presented in figure 1 depicts stature as the product of an *environment* comprised of multiple forces that influence the exchange of resources between colleges and universities and different constituencies; *inputs* in the form of constituents' needs and expectations for educational programs and services, which carry stimuli from the environment to the institution and induce decisions about programs and resources; *attributes of organization and performance* that facilitate or retard institutional responsiveness to external constituencies by influencing important decisions related to domains of activity; a *conversion process* that transforms constituents' needs and expectations and environmental stimuli into decisions about programs and resources; *outputs* that carry the results of institutional programs and services (i.e., benefits) to multiple constituencies in the environment; *communication* that involves formal and informal procedures for disseminating information about outputs to important constituencies; and *feedback* that transmits public perceptions about the outputs produced by an institution in one period back to the conversion process (and ultimately to the external environment) as the inputs in a later period. All of these dimensions interact with one another. Together they produce stature for an institution, or a set of institutions, in the form of constituents' perceptions of convergence between conditions, needs, and stimuli in the environment and the benefits produced by institutions through educational programs and services.

With the model as a framework for analysis, it is possible to illustrate more precisely the dimensions of stature. Scholars and practitioners have long been interested in investigating the attributes of colleges and universities that contribute to prestige (Astin 1982; Astin and Solmon 1979; Kuh 1981). A host of

FIGURE 1
MODEL OF INSTITUTIONAL STATURE

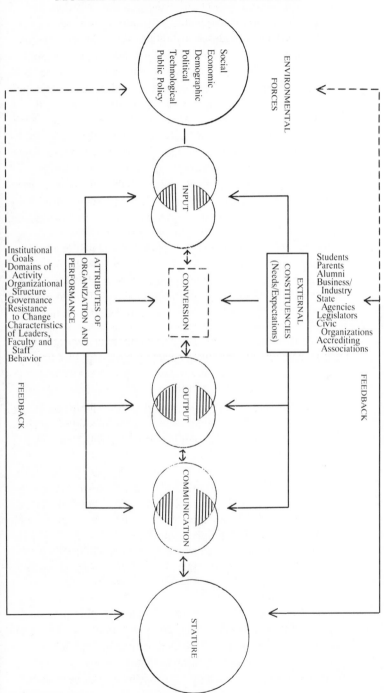

factors have been identified: the test scores of entering students, the quality of the faculty, expenditures per student, size of the endowment, number of volumes in the library, admissions selectivity, volume of private gifts and grants, accomplishments of alumni, quality of campus facilities, size of the operating budget, peer rankings of program quality, reputation for innovation, and the quality of leadership. While all of these factors contribute to stature in some way, in the aggregate they do not make up stature. Certainly factors like the quality of faculty and the leadership provided by the president are important elements in the achievement of stature. These factors, however, relate exclusively to institutionally determined dimensions of stature—those that can be identified and controlled by faculty and administrators. They do not account for dimensions implicit in the model that lie outside institutional control—namely, societal forces and the public's needs and expectations. To better understand the multiple dimensions of stature that must be considered, it is appropriate to think of colleges and universities as service organizations operating on multiple axes (Drucker 1973), which represent variations among institutions in time, service region, mission, benefits/costs, and public perception (see figure 2). At their confluence is stature, which is the product of interaction among the axes. For example, it is possible to view stature as:

- the cumulative product of historical benefits rendered over a long period of time to a broad array of constituencies by an institution with a comprehensive mission (traditional prestige);
- the capacity of a college with a comprehensive mission to produce benefits that meet or exceed the expectations of specific constituencies in a local service region by reducing the gap between individual circumstances and prevailing societal conditions (satisfaction);
- the performance of a college with a comprehensive mission in affecting constituencies over time through communications describing the benefits of investment in education (affect).

A few select institutions have been able to combine historical production of desirable benefits and continuing favorable public perception to promulgate a form of stature known as "traditional prestige." For example, a pervasive mystique is associ-

FIGURE 2

AXES DETERMINING VARIATION IN STATURE AMONG COLLEGES AND UNIVERSITIES

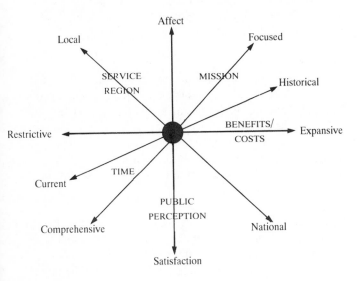

ated with Harvard University. Viewed from its modest beginning in 1636 to the present, Harvard has been described as a multinational academic conglomerate, the think tank of all think tanks, and a power center of astounding impact that penetrates every institution in American society (Lopez 1979). "The Harvard mystique is a strong reality that carries a powerful effect on American life . . . what is left to question is whether Harvard is worthy of the power it possesses" (Lopez 1979).

Also to be considered is the matter of a stature of distinctiveness. Berea College has stature in educating Appalachia's poor, Morehouse College has stature in educating black male students, Carnegie-Mellon and MIT have stature in computer science, and Oberlin has stature in music. Institutions like Rice University and Smith College have stature implicit in the size of their endowments, and the University of Notre Dame has stature that is not measured by the usual yardsticks. Such institutions have an "organizational saga" or an institutional mythos that permeates the campus.

Other colleges and universities are new to the ranks of institutions holding stature. They have had to undertake special programs and resource initiatives to build stature. A good example is the University of Texas, which in the late 1970s and early 1980s made an effort to enter the circle of the nation's elite universities by attracting nationally recognized scholars in diverse disciplines. A number of institutions, perhaps the majority, have been unable to develop stature to any significant degree with multiple publics.

Summary

Institutional stature has multiple dimensions that can be examined in the context of a systems model. As a concept, stature supersedes the boundaries of any single factor or combination of factors. Its forms of expression are as diverse as the spectrum of postsecondary institutions in the United States.

The primary value of the working definition, systems model, and model dimensions of stature rests in the questions they pose that guide analysis:

1. What is the relationship among prevailing environmental forces (demographic and economic trends, social issues, technological change, public policy), public needs and expectations for postsecondary education, and the public's perception of college and university stature?
2. What effect(s), if any, do the structure and functioning of the academic organization have on college and university stature? Do they serve to enhance stature, to diminish stature, or to vary, in effect depending on the organizational attribute(s) in question?
3. What strategies and practices are currently being used in complex organizations (including colleges and universities) to alter domains of activity and outputs to enhance stature?
4. What strategies and practices currently not in use in colleges and universities need to be adapted to enhance stature?

If colleges and universities are to enhance their stature in a period of rapid social, economic, demographic, and technological change in the 1990s, significant strategies must be developed. Without specific action, most institutions will find themselves the target of continuing criticism by external publics, ranging from students and parents making decisions about enrollment to government agencies making decisions about financial appropriations.

CHANGING PUBLIC ATTITUDES TOWARD HIGHER EDUCATION

The next two sections examine certain specific dimensions of stature in depth: forces in the environment that affect the goals and performance of colleges and universities; the interests and expectations of constituents that influence public opinion about higher education; and organizational attributes and characteristics that facilitate or retard an institution's responsiveness to external forces and to public opinion. Two questions implicit in the model are the focus of examination: What is the influence on institutional stature stemming from societal conditions and individual attitudes and opinions toward higher education? How do organizational attributes of colleges and universities affect stature?

[There was] a decline in the public's confidence in the leaders of major educational institutions between 1966 and 1984.

Societal Conditions and Public Opinion

The general tenor of national reports published in the late 1940s indicated that people had no quarrel with colleges. They wanted more of them, they wanted more young people to go, and they admired professors. They were not unduly critical of curricula, and they were willing to give instructors quite a lot of freedom.

This approving public attitude toward higher education continued into and throughout the Golden Era of higher education (1955 to 1970). At that time, not enough qualified individuals were available to fill the needs of the labor market resulting from a high wartime mortality rate, a low wartime birth rate, and the enormous postwar demand of modernizing businesses and industries for trained personnel. Throughout this period, the general public viewed postsecondary education as a key to social and economic mobility. Enrollments grew steadily, and the stature of colleges and universities remained steady or rose in the public's eye. The confidence of the general public in colleges and universities, as in other social institutions, however, diminished between 1965 and 1985, a period of time in which pressures for accountability made the public and elected officials look critically at higher education. Several phenomena give evidence of this trend:

The analysis of societal conditions and public opinion presented in this section was developed through examination of popular journals and opinion surveys published between 1965 and 1985. The assistance of Mary L. Hummel in reviewing and synthesizing information is acknowledged.

1. A general lowering of the certifying effect of higher education degrees. Only in certain exceptional cases, such as the elite research universities, has the public continued to view the certifying effect as considerable (de l'Ain 1981).
2. Increased discrepancies in the certifying effect among colleges and universities. The degrees conferred by prestigious institutions in a changing economy provide advantages to clients in relationships with social institutions (Parsons and Platt 1972).
3. A decline in the public's confidence in the leaders of major educational institutions between 1966 and 1984, as documented in public opinion polls (Louis Harris and Associates 1984).

A 1984 Harris survey (1,247 adults nationwide) showed that only 40 percent of those surveyed had a great deal of confidence in the leaders of colleges and universities. In 1961, the figure was 61 percent. This reversal in public opinion has prompted some college and university leaders to call for new efforts to build public support. Speaking before a national assembly of the Council for Advancement and Support of Education, Harvard's Derek Bok identified the current challenge to higher education as "not merely a challenge of public relations, but a challenge of substance that should be treated as such" (*Chronicle of Higher Education* 22 July 1987).

Environmental forces and public needs, expectations, and attitudes are important dimensions of college and university stature. Mindful of the fact that colleges and universities cannot easily influence the tempo of societal change and public opinion, educational policy makers are nevertheless surprised when contradictions occur in expected relationships. Would it be logical, for example, to expect that college and university enrollments would continue to rise in the face of a projected downturn in traditional college-age students? Or would it logically follow that the majority of the American public believes that a college education is more important than ever at a time when colleges are encountering difficulty in attracting funds from alumni, pessimism mounts in Congress, and the general public is increasingly skeptical about costs (Media General 1987)? Societal conditions and public opinion are important forces in determining stature. They require careful analysis if faculty and administrators are to understand how stature develops and how it can be enhanced.

The following discussion examines societal conditions and public opinion as input factors in determining stature. The underlying premise is that perception of college and university stature varies in accord with changes in societal conditions and public opinion. National surveys of public opinion, when combined with analysis of prevailing social conditions in specific time periods, provide a crude index of public attitudes toward higher education. This index can be presented in the form of a capsule description of trends in societal conditions and public opinion at five-year intervals between 1965 and 1985.

To facilitate analysis, two dimensions of public opinion toward higher education are presented for each time frame: (1) public attitudes toward social institutions reflected in survey data, and (2) national survey data describing public perceptions of colleges and universities. Concepts of psychological well-being and ill-being are then introduced to explain variation in opinion among individuals and groups associated with changing societal conditions. Finally, a series of postulates explain variation in public opinion as a function of change in individual latitudes of acceptance and rejection applied to higher education during periods of societal transition.

Changing Public Attitudes and Perceptions
1965–1970
Societal conditions. In the mid-1960s, economic prosperity was on the rise with record growth in auto production, steel, capital spending, personal income, and corporate profits. Unemployment fell to 4.1 percent, while college enrollment increased by 12.2 percent in 1964–65. Concurrent with the commitment of the United States to the Vietnam War, college graduates faced the largest starting salaries ever offered by business and industry. The focus of legislation was on social security, health care, medicare benefits, and environmental pollution.

In 1967, violence erupted in American cities, and disparate incomes between social groups brought on the loss of unifying purpose and a tide of frustration. The president's popularity declined and inflationary signs (federal deficit, rising interest rates, and pressure on the dollar) appeared as the economy began to weaken. The Scholastic Aptitude Test came under attack, and college attendance became the norm as public colleges and universities experienced unprecedented growth in enrollments. New two-year colleges opened at a rate of 65 per year, students demanded more attention to teaching, and colleges began to spend time and resources on public service as a method to address social problems.

The 1960s closed with a nation divided and demoralized by the Vietnam War. Campus unrest and violence in the cities worsened, and patriotism surfaced in the middle class as a counterpart to wide-ranging attacks to public- and private-sector institutions. Strikes by public employees became commonplace. Richard Nixon was elected to the presidency on a platform of law and order. On college and university campuses, faculty sought academic reforms and curricular relevance to social change. The growing impatience of the public with campus disorder widened the gap between the academic world and the larger community.

Public opinion. Does a relationship exist between discontent and public opinion toward social institutions? Survey research data describing public opinion reveal that confidence in major social institutions in American society declined steadily between 1965 and 1970. Surveys conducted annually by Louis Harris and Associates between 1967 and 1971 show that public confidence in the leaders of nine major social institutions decreased from an average of 43 percent expressing a "great deal of confidence" in 1966 to 27 percent expressing the same amount of confidence in 1971 (Louis Harris and Associates 1978). The greatest declines were noted for the military, major companies, and colleges and universities.

Although efforts to link change in public opinion with change in societal conditions are a risky venture at best, public opinion experts attributed the decline in public confidence in colleges and universities between 1965 and 1970 to unrest on campuses and growing skepticism about the capacity of faculty and administrators to control aggressive behavior that would be considered criminal in general society (Louis Harris and Associates 1978). Bills introduced into state legislatures to curb campus disorder, although unenforceable and unconstitutional, drew widespread public support. Demands for accountability rose among specific social groups outside colleges and universities—the young and middle aged, the highly educated, whites, and those living in or near metropolitan centers—as explanations for campus unrest and justifications for tolerance of disorder failed to gain support (Kleiman and Clemente 1976). At the same time, the public felt that favorable economic conditions were beginning to deteriorate as inflation heated up and unemployment rose.

In sum, public confidence in college and university leaders appeared to decline as questions were raised about the capacity of campuses to control student unrest, to address the harmful effects of economic downturn, and to demonstrate accountability in relationship to public needs and expectations. Increasingly, colleges and universities became the target of public skepticism about their capacity to alleviate social problems. They no longer carried the status of sacrosanct institutions in American society.

1971–1975

Societal conditions. The 1970s began with renewed unrest on the campuses and the shootings at Kent State University. In 1972, 18-year-olds got the vote, the structure of the American family changed rapidly, and young couples lived together outside marriage. Youth lived in communes. Rebellion against authority was a widespread attitude among youth. A mass exodus occurred from rural to metropolitan areas. Nixon withdrew troops from Vietnam while moving to open dialogue with China. Heavy government controls were placed on the economy—most wages, prices, rents, and dividends were controlled—and a 10 percent surcharge was applied to imports. Unemployment stood at 6.2 percent in 1972. The public mood shifted to increased conservatism in reaction to the counterculture of the 1960s and excessive welfare spending. The Watergate break-in in 1972 and the oil crisis and sudden oil shortage in 1973 crippled the nation and led to a general crisis of authority and trust.

Richard Nixon resigned in 1974, and a prolonged economic recession began. The national output of goods and services declined by 7.5 percent in the last quarter of 1974, new car sales plunged 26 percent below the previous year, and unemployment rose to 7.1 percent. New York City teetered on the brink of bankruptcy in 1975, and Congress passed an energy bill to allow oil prices to rise as a method of increasing supply. By the close of 1975, antigovernment conservatism became the party line of stature-seeking politicians, and Jimmy Carter was soon to be elected president. Unemployment stood at 8.3 percent; the United States was struggling to recover from a depression, the Vietnam War, and the Watergate break-in. The mood of the public was one of concern about moral leadership, simplicity, and the direction of social institutions.

Colleges and universities moved to implement reforms in undergraduate education in response to students' calls for change in the structure and content of curricula. Grading standards and course requirements were relaxed, pass-fail options were introduced, plans for "universities without walls" were developed, and new courses were introduced into the curriculum to satisfy special interest groups.

Public opinion. Public opinion surveys conducted between 1971 and 1975 showed selective decline in the public's confidence in the leaders of social institutions. The level of confidence in leaders increased for some institutions (television news and the press), while it decreased for others (the military, major companies, Congress, and the executive branch of federal government) and remained stable for a third group (colleges and universities, the U.S. Supreme Court, organized religion, and organized labor). A 1975 Harris survey showed 55 percent of the general public indicating that college and university leaders "really know what people want" (see table 1), which compared favorably to most organized groups and institutions. Public attention centered on military, industrial, and political leaders as an important force in the nation's economy.

Labor, government, military, and business and industry leaders were viewed as having difficulty comprehending the changing values and aspirations that had taken over the country. Serious and constructive approaches to problems of inflation, recession, energy, and other issues having to do with the quality of American life were lacking but necessary. College and university leaders were credited with understanding students' and faculty members' aspirations as reflected in curriculum reforms, changing academic requirements, and new instructional delivery systems (Louis Harris and Associates 1975). Questions mounted, however, about the value and costs of higher education. In a 1974 replicated study of survey research on public attitudes toward higher education originally conducted by the Institute for Social Research in 1963, the National Opinion Research Center found important strands of change in the public's perception of colleges and universities. Between 1963 and 1974, it was discovered that:

TABLE 1

PUBLIC PERCEPTION OF LEADERS' CAPACITY TO KNOW WHAT PEOPLE WANT (PERCENT)

	Really Know What People Want	Mostly Out of Touch	Not Sure
People running for office	69	21	10
Television news	66	24	10
Banks	64	24	12
The press	59	29	12
Colleges and universities	55	34	11
Local government	47	40	13
State government	46	41	13
Organized labor	45	39	16
Law firms	45	38	17
Organized religion	44	40	16
Major companies	39	50	11
The military	38	44	18
The U.S. Supreme Court	38	43	19
The White House	35	51	14
The executive branch of the federal government	34	50	16
Congress	34	54	12

Source: Louis Harris and Associates 1975.

1. A smaller percentage of the public in 1974 thought it was "more" important for a high school graduate to go to college than it was 10 years earlier (82 percent compared to 96 percent).
2. A larger percentage of the public thought "young people are in some ways not so good after going to college" (55 percent in 1974 compared to 42 percent in 1963).
3. A smaller percentage of the public in 1974 thought "it would be a good thing for this country if more students could go to college than go now" (66 percent compared to 82 percent).
4. A larger percentage of the public thought "the country spent too much money on higher education and too many young people were attending college" in 1974 (19 percent) compared to 1963 (5 percent).

Thus, the coalescence of powerful events (economic depression, Watergate, and the oil crisis) tainted the public's confidence in all social institutions, including higher education. Change in the expression of public confidence was most prominent for institutions viewed as having a direct link with the economy, the oil crisis, or Watergate. Colleges and universities concentrated on activities that would build public support rather than criticism—development of new curricula, public service initiatives, and students' involvement in decision making. The line between campus and community grew thinner as a result of those efforts. As the costs of college attendance continued to increase and barriers between town and gown began to erode, efforts escalated to bring new standards of accountability to colleges and universities (Hechinger 1977). Public opinion toward higher education was dualistic, reflecting, on the one hand, satisfaction with efforts to improve the relevance of education to external groups and, on the other, dissatisfaction with rising costs.

1976–1980

Societal conditions. Jimmy Carter was elected president in 1976. For the first time in more than 12 years, the nation was at peace abroad and at home. The crime rate declined, and birth and marriage rates rose in 1977. Charities reported sharp increases in donations. Financial aid policies came under review as efforts were made to offset rising tuition costs. Voluntary wage and price restraints were imposed in 1978, setting the stage for confrontations between labor and management. By 1979, labor negotiations were under way in the rubber, textile, electrical, and automobile industries, and buyers' dependence on foreign products as a method to restrain prices had begun to increase. The public sentiment favored balancing the federal budget through outlawing deficit spending. When Ronald Reagan was elected president in 1980, pressure for immigration was massive. Violence erupted in cities like Miami as explosive growth of the immigrant population changed the fabric of relationships among social groups and civic authorities. Interest rates approached a record high of 20 percent during the first quarter of 1980 but declined to 11 percent by the summer. The consumer became sovereign in postsecondary education as colleges implemented new marketing strategies to offset the decline in high school graduates. Disparities between public and private institutions of higher education intensified as colleges and universities engaged in head-to-head competition for students and resources.

Public opinion. When Ronald Reagan prepared to take office in November 1980, public confidence in the leadership of social institutions hovered just above the all-time lows recorded during previous years. The number of citizens expressing a great deal of confidence in the major institutions was so low that social institutions were struggling to maintain any real credibility with the publics they served. A Harris survey of a cross-section of 1,199 adults in November 1980 revealed that public confidence in the leaders of major social institutions declined steadily between 1977 and 1980 (see table 2). Only 16 percent of the population expressed a great deal of confidence in leaders running major corporations—down from 23 percent who felt that way in 1977 and 55 percent in 1966 (Louis Harris and Associates 1980). Similar declines between 1977 and 1980 and 1966 and 1980 were noted for medicine, the Supreme Court, organized religion, the executive branch of the federal government, the military, and higher education institutions. For all social institutions, the highest ratings were assigned to college and university leaders, with 36 percent of the public expressing "high confidence."

A 1978 survey of public confidence in major social institutions by the National Opinion Research Center disclosed findings similar to the Harris survey. The percentage of the population expressing a great deal of confidence in the leaders running social institutions had declined since the early and mid-1970s to the following levels in 1978: medicine—45 percent, organized religion—38 percent, the military—31 percent, major companies—31 percent, education—29 percent, the U.S. Supreme Court—23 percent, the executive branch of the federal government—13 percent, and organized labor—12 percent. When data were refined to examine subgroups' perceptions of confidence in the leaders of educational institutions, interesting differences emerged among the groups. A greater percentage of persons in the age group 50 and older (32 percent) expressed high confidence in educational leaders, compared to persons 18 to 24 years (29 percent). Among whites, the percentage expressing high confidence was 27 percent, whereas for non-whites it was 42 percent. And college graduates were less apt to feel confident about educational leaders than those with less than a high school education.

College graduates were less apt to feel confident about educational leaders than those with less than a high school education.

TABLE 2
HIGH CONFIDENCE IN LEADERS OF SOCIAL INSTITUTIONS (PERCENT)

	11/80	2/79	8/78	11/77	3/76	3/75	9/74	9/73	2/66
Higher education institutions	36	33	41	41	31	36	40	44	61
Medicine	34	30	42	55	42	x	49	57	73
Television news	29	37	35	30	28	34	32	41	x
The military	28	29	29	31	23	25	29	40	61
The U.S. Supreme Court	27	28	29	31	22	x	34	33	50
Organized religion	22	20	34	34	24	x	32	36	41
The press	19	28	23	19	20	24	25	30	29
Congress	18	18	10	15	9	11	16	x	42
The White House	18	15	14	26	11	13	18	18	x
The executive branch of the federal government	17	17	14	23	11	x	18	19	41
Major companies	16	18	22	23	16	18	15	29	55
Organized labor	14	10	15	15	10	16	18	20	22
Law firms	13	16	18	16	12	x	17	24	x

x = Not asked
Source: Louis Harris and Associates 1980.

In summary, 1976–1980 witnessed a continuing decline in public opinion toward social institutions and the accentuation of groups' differences in attitudes toward higher education. Insular thoughts and actions were the watchwords of the times, as changing economic, political, and social conditions forced consumers to look inward for meaningful interpretations of events and circumstances. Growing frustration with the economy and the labor market precipitated questions about the value of a college degree. Lacking reliable data about student outcomes in work and further education, college officials provided only partial answers to questions about benefits and costs, thereby adding to the public's skepticism. Faced with mounting calls for accountability and reform and cognizant of dire economic and demographic forecasts, college administrators embraced marketing and planning strategies to alter the direction of public opinion and to improve resources.

1981–1985

Societal conditions. The first year of the Reagan Administration began with substantial budget cuts, slowing the growth of federal spending and shrinking the amount of revenue to social programs by 23 percent. A three-year cut in income taxes was passed, resulting in reduction in the size of government and stimulation of productivity in the private sector to curb inflation. Management achieved the upper hand in labor relations, and unemployment rose to 9 percent in the last quarter of 1981. By July 1982, unemployment had increased to 11 percent and interest rates were beginning to decline, stimulating increased sales of stocks and bonds. With improved corporate production in 1983, unemployment fell, personal income rose, and the rate of inflation declined. The federal deficit began to balloon and interest rates increased as government requirements for credit expanded in proportion to the deficit. Technological change in different sectors of the labor market altered the approach to management and thinned the labor force as inefficient plants were closed and obsolete jobs eliminated. The economy diversified to include a new emphasis on service and high- and low-technology industries. Disparities among levels of income and education for different population groups loomed on the horizon as a significant social issue. By 1985, the federal budget deficit had risen to $200 billion, American farmers were awash in red ink as farm foreclosures became more common, and the focus of the federal government shifted to consideration of alternative policies to reduce the budget deficit. Curriculum reform became a subject of importance for colleges and universities, following a succession of national reports describing aging postsecondary education facilities and staff and fragmented undergraduate curriculum.

Public opinion. Public confidence in the leaders of major social institutions rose steadily between 1980 and 1985. A 1984 Harris survey of a cross-section of 1,247 adults nationwide indicated the largest increase in public confidence in the leaders of social institutions in a one-year period (1983–84) since 1966 (see table 3). Although the level of public confidence in institutions remained well below what it was in the mid-60s, the percentage of the public expressing high confidence in the leaders of 12 social institutions between 1980 and 1984 rose six points. Public confidence in college and university leaders gained four

TABLE 3
CONFIDENCE IN LEADERS OF SOCIAL INSTITUTIONS (PERCENT)

	1984	1983	1982	1981	1980	1979	1978	1977	1976	1975	1974	1973	1972	1971	1966
The military	45	35	31	28	28	29	29	27	23	24	33	40	35	27	61
Medicine	43	35	32	37	34	30	42	43	42	43	50	57	48	61	73
The White House	42	23	20	28	18	15	13	31	11	x	28	18	x	x	x
Major educational institutions, such as colleges and universities	40	36	30	34	36	33	41	37	31	36	40	44	33	37	61
The U.S. Supreme Court	35	33	25	29	27	28	29	29	22	28	40	33	28	23	50
Congress	28	20	13	16	18	18	10	17	9	13	18	x	21	19	42
TV news	28	24	24	24	29	37	35	28	28	35	31	41	x	x	x
Organized religion	24	22	20	22	22	20	34	29	24	32	32	36	30	27	41
State governments	23	18	x	x	x	x	15	18	16	x	x	24	x	x	x
Local governments	23	18	x	x	x	x	19	18	21	x	x	28	x	x	x
Major companies	19	18	18	16	16	18	22	20	16	19	21	29	27	23	55
The press	18	19	14	16	19	28	23	18	20	26	25	30	18	18	29
Law firms	17	12	x	x	13	16	18	14	12	16	18	24	x	x	x
Organized labor	12	10	8	12	14	10	15	14	10	14	18	20	15	14	22

x = Not asked
Source: Louis Harris and Associates 1984.

percentage points between 1980 and 1984 while falling to fourth position in confidence ratings behind the military, medicine, and the White House. In 1984, 40 percent of the population expressed a high level of confidence in college and university leaders compared to 36 percent in 1980 and 61 percent in 1966.

Data for a Gallup poll collected in 1983 and 1985 from a random sample of 1,528 adults nationwide revealed that a growing number of citizens assigned high value to higher education. Ninety-one percent believed a college education was "very important" or "fairly important," compared to 89 percent who responded that way in 1983 and 82 percent who did so in 1978. Only 7 percent indicated a college education was "not too important" (Gallup 1985).

Surveys conducted by Group Attitudes Corporation between 1982 and 1984 to determine how adults in the United States viewed colleges and universities revealed different perceptions of postsecondary education, depending on group characteristics. More than one half (54 percent) of an unweighted random sample of 1,188 adults 18 years of age and older throughout the United States believed that the knowledge gained in college is "very important" for later life. Another 37 percent thought a college education is "somewhat important" for later life, while only 2 percent thought it is "not at all important." When attention shifted to public opinion about the overall quality of college education in the United States between 1982 and 1984—the period immediately preceding the development and release of sponsored reports assessing the condition of higher education—the results were mixed. In 1982, 72.5 percent rated the overall quality of a college education "excellent" or "good." In 1983, the comparable proportion was 68.1 percent and in 1984, 66.9 percent. The number of individuals who rated the quality of a college education as excellent in 1984 (15.6 percent) increased slightly, however, compared to the proportion (13.5 percent) who did so in 1983.

Over four out of every 10 respondents in 1984 believed that the quality of a college education in the United States was generally improving (43.5 percent), and 32.6 percent believed it was staying about the same (see table 4)—a sharp increase over 1983, when 36 percent believed the quality of a college education was getting better, and 36.5 percent felt it was staying about the same. In 1983, 16.7 percent believed that the quality of a college education was getting worse. In 1984, the compa-

TABLE 4
IS THE QUALITY OF A COLLEGE EDUCATION GETTING BETTER OR WORSE?
(Weighted N = 1,005)

	Generally Improving 43.5%	Staying About the Same 32.6%	Generally Declining 13.3%	Don't Know/ No Opinion 10.6%
Total				
Income Level				
Less than $15,000	37.6	36.2	14.6	11.7
$15,000 to $24,999	46.7	33.0	9.8	10.5
$25,000 to $39,999	44.6	28.5	19.3	7.6
$40,000 or more	41.7	36.2	13.4	9.4
Education Level				
No college	43.4	33.0	11.8	11.8
Some college	44.8	32.0	13.8	9.9
College graduate	42.0	32.0	18.2	9.9
Region				
New England	40.9	36.4	10.6	12.1
Middle Atlantic	42.2	38.0	11.8	8.0
South Atlantic	43.7	32.1	15.3	8.4
East South Central	48.1	34.2	7.6	11.4
West South Central	48.8	23.8	13.8	12.5
East North Central	40.5	32.9	16.2	10.5
West North Central	45.9	32.4	10.8	10.8
Mountain	52.6	18.4	13.2	15.8
Pacific	39.5	30.9	16.0	14.8
Sex				
Female	42.6	33.5	12.1	11.9
Male	44.8	31.4	14.9	9.0

Question: Would you say the overall quality of college education is generally improving, getting better . . . , staying about the same, not really changing at all . . . , generally declining, getting worse?

Source: Group Attitudes Corporation 1984.

rable proportion was 13.3 percent. Individuals who had graduated from college were more apt to feel that the quality of a college education had declined (18.2 percent) than those who had been to college but had not earned a bachelor's degree (13.8 percent) or those who had never gone to college (11.8 percent). Individuals who earned between $25,000 and $40,000 a year also were highly critical of the quality of a college education, with 19.3 percent contending that quality had decreased, compared to 15.7 percent in 1983.

In sum, dual forces of economic growth and technological change sparked improvement in consumers' confidence. Public confidence in the leaders of most social institutions rose dramatically between 1981 and 1985. Higher education leaders ranked fourth behind leaders in the military, medicine, and the White House in confidence ratings. With the economy on the upswing, inflation under control, and knowledge of technology important for mobility in the labor market, college attendance became an important investment in the future. Although doubts lingered as to the quality of a college education, educational attainment had become the key to financial security in the minds of many college-age and adult learners.

Psychological Well-Being and Ill-Being

Projecting institutional stature as a product of the relationship between prevailing societal conditions and public opinion is characterized by a high degree of uncertainty. Public sentiment toward social institutions and leaders will invariably generalize to colleges and universities unless decision makers are able to cultivate a perception of distinctiveness that places higher education on a higher plane than other institutions. Sociological theory provides some insights into how this phenomenon occurs.

Individuals react positively or negatively to colleges and universities based on their affective feeling in response to societal conditions and their cognitive impressions of satisfaction or dissatisfaction that color impressions of objects and events—what might be called "psychological well-being or ill-being" (Campbell 1981). Conventional thinking generally assumes that a close and predictable relationship exists between the quality of objective circumstances in which individuals live and the quality of their subjective experience (Campbell 1981; Campbell, Converse, and Rogers 1976; McKennell 1978; U.S. Department of HEW 1969). Well-being is a reflection of objective

conditions: the average family income, the number of houses and automobiles owned, the number of children in schools and colleges, the average length of the work week, the capacity to acquire and pay for quality health care, the amount of income available for discretionary purchases. Institutions that contribute to the acquisition of goods and services serve as an instrument through which individuals enhance their feelings of well-being (Campbell 1981). Colleges and universities contribute to well-being by sponsoring academic degree programs, the successful completion of which propels students into higher-paying jobs that ultimately lead to improved socioeconomic circumstances.

The relationship between the affluence of socioeconomic circumstances and well-being is not always direct, however. Individuals respond to societal conditions and features of the environment, not within the limits of their objective reality but as they are perceived. The perceptual field of the individual contains a mixture of facilitating and inhibiting conditions that influence the capacity to achieve a sense of well-being and to view institutions positively. Over the last 20 years, income has tended to lose its force as an indicator of well-being, especially among college-educated citizens (Campbell 1981). Numerous research studies have shown that as a society becomes more affluent, a smaller number of individuals will achieve a sense of well-being through favorable objective circumstances (Barnes and Inglehart 1974; Lane 1978; Scitovsky 1976; Walster, Walster, and Berscheid 1978). Studies of the populations of seven European countries reported a "shift from a primary concern with material well-being and physical security toward greater emphasis on the quality of life and self-realization" with increasing affluence (Barnes and Inglehart 1974).

Despite the general consensus reflected in research on the relationship of objective circumstances and psychological well-being, a debate continues as to the effect of societal change on individual needs and perceptions of social institutions. For example, students entering American colleges and universities in Fall 1984 and after—a time of continuing economic growth, advancing technology, structural change in the labor market, changing family structure, and the rise of social issues like structural unemployment, generational poverty, and unequal incomes—have undergone a change in values from altruism to self-aggrandizement (Astin et al. 1985). Of a sample of 182,370 new freshmen at 345 colleges and universities participating in the Cooperative Institutional Research Program, more students than ever in the 19 years of the program (67.8 percent) indicated a "very important" reason for attending college in 1984 was to be able to make more money (Astin et al. 1985). The survey data also revealed that 71.2 percent of the freshmen, when asked what objectives they considered important, said they hoped to be "well off" financially.

This information raises questions about determinants of college and university stature in periods of social change. Is stature a function of favorable perceptions of the capacity of higher education to produce benefits that improve objective circumstances in life? Is it a reflection of institutional capacity to facilitate self-realization through improvement in the quality of life during periods of economic prosperity? Is it a function of public perception of distinctiveness in goals, operations, and performance that distinguishes colleges and universities from other types of organizations? Is stature a function of all of these factors working in combination to contribute to a certain "fundamental trust" in higher education?

Postulates Derived from Research
Analysis of public opinion survey data in the context of changing societal conditions leads to a series of postulates that further understanding of stature in colleges and universities. Although these postulates are derived primarily from examining higher education as a social institution, they also can be applied to local institutions.

1. Individuals and groups react to colleges and universities as they see them, not as they objectively are. Perceptions of institutional stature are influenced by the values, expectations, experience, and personality traits individuals bring to the situation.
2. Institutional stature is an attitude or perception that derives in part from an individual's views of his or her contemporary situation. It depends on the subjective characteristics of the individual (age, level of education, income, et cetera) and objective characteristics of the situation (time, place, societal conditions, and so on).
3. Institutional stature is comprised of two components— "satisfaction/dissatisfaction" and "positive and negative affect." A positive opinion expressed by important constituencies in relationship to information published by colleges and universities describing the success of graduates

in attaining higher-paying jobs is an aspect of positive or negative affect. Satisfaction and affect are related, but they are not identical; in some circumstances, they may move in opposite directions.

4. Satisfaction/dissatisfaction is a function of the gap an individual perceives between prevailing societal conditions, his or her needs and expectations, and institutional performance in producing benefits that satisfy needs.
Changes in level of satisfaction may result from change in societal conditions, change in individual needs and expectations, change in institutional performance, or all three. The degree and direction of change may influence perceptions held by the individual of institutional stature.

5. Affect reflects the spontaneous feelings of interest, disinterest, or antipathy associated with events in the individual's immediate experience. These events are both positively and negatively toned, and their sum determines the individual's perception of institutional stature.

6. Satisfaction and affect are necessary preconditions for stature. The absence of either condition will serve to constrain stature in colleges and universities. The absence of both conditions will effectively negate the perception of stature.

In sum, public perception of the stature of colleges and universities is a product of satisfaction and positive affect determined by societal conditions, individual needs and expectations, and institutional performance. As the first dimension in the systems model, societal conditions have a discernible impact on public opinion. Although not easily explained in a cause-and-effect relationship with public opinion, sensitivity on the part of faculty and administrators to a relationship of this type is important. They should also understand the relationship between societal conditions and other dimensions in the systems model—attributes of the academic organization and domains of institutional activity (performance) affecting outputs—to achieve a better understanding of how stature develops and how it can be improved.

ATTRIBUTES OF ACADEMIC ORGANIZATION AND PERFORMANCE

The academic organization of colleges and universities always has had an acknowledged effect on the relationship of the institution to its external environment, yet certain properties of the academic organization resist change (Baldridge 1980; March 1982; Pfeffer and Salancik 1978; Weick 1978. Viewed in the systems model presented in figure 1, the academic organization is a loosely coupled structure that receives, filters, and acts (inaction is a form of action) on cues coming from the external environment. Specific attributes (goals, activity domains, governance, management practices, academic policies, and so on) facilitate or impede institutional responses to external cues, thereby determining stature by shaping the relationship between the institution and important constituencies in its environment.

The problem with this portrait is that colleges and universities cannot be viewed as rational organizations.

The literature on complex organizations reveals how institutions change their activity domains to improve their relationship to the external environment and the effect of those changes on organizational stature and performance in periods of changing social values and customs. For example, while the YMCA was originally evangelical and religious in nature, as American society secularized, so also did the organization, emphasizing more the recreational and educational activities of its operations (Zald and Denton 1963). An examination of the Tennessee Valley Authority's history also reveals the alteration of activity domains to enhance stature and to obtain public support (Selznick 1949). Changing public expectations that antiquate institutional activity domains and that appear inimical to the professional interests of college faculty and staff have frequently been the focus of institutional efforts to reconfigure activities to match external needs and expectations (Dowling and Pfeffer 1975). In recent years, colleges and universities have moved to implement innovative curricula (weekend colleges, continuing education, distance learning, community-based education, for example) and marketing strategies to stabilize enrollment and to attract resources (Hilpert and Alfred 1987). In this process, the implicit goal of completing a degree in the structured activity of academic programs has been deemphasized in favor of flexible programs to accommodate increasing numbers of adult learners.

In theory, colleges and universities are rational institutions organized to meet the educational needs and expectations of individuals, groups, and organizations through a hierarchical system to bring action in a comprehensible social structure (March 1982). The problem with this portrait is that colleges and universities cannot be viewed as rational organizations. The domains of activity pursued by faculty and administrators do not necessarily reflect common goals, nor do they center exclusively on the satisfaction of public expectations. Faculty and administrators act on the basis of limited comprehension of the external environment. They are boundedly rational rather than completely rational. They have incomplete information and modest capabilities for processing information (March 1982). They pursue self-interests that may or may not be congruent with the goals of the organization. They are part of an organization that is responsive to public expectations but also insulated from these expectations by virtue of organizational characteristics like goal ambiguity, professionalism, problematic technology, and environmental vulnerability (Baldridge et al. 1978).

Distinguishing Characteristics of the Academic Organization
What are some distinguishing attributes of the academic organization? What role do they play in determining stature in colleges and universities? And how are academic institutions similar to or different from other types of organizations? Similar to other organizations, colleges and universities have goals, hierarchical systems and structures, decision-making processes, and a bureaucratic administration that handles routine business. Unlike other organizations, however, they face continuing problems with vague, ambiguous goals, technology, and decision processes. They must grapple with a high degree of conflict and uncertainty in a loosely coupled organization (Weick 1978). Colleges and universities maintain responsiveness but also insularity in relationship to the publics they serve. Faculty require autonomy in work and maintain divided loyalties within the institution (Katz and Kahn 1978). They believe that only peers can judge their performance, and they reject the evaluations of others, even those who are technically their superiors in the organizational hierarchy (Baldridge et al. 1978). These characteristics undercut the capacity of the institution for quick response to changing needs. Over time they channel output and determine satisfaction and affect among multiple publics interacting in specific ways with the institution.

The outputs produced by academic organizations are not necessarily compatible with the needs and expectations of the publics served. Inactivity and insulation prevail among the faculty in academic organizations. Most faculty find management and policy making uninteresting and unrewarding activities that are better left to administrators (Baldridge 1971; Mortimer and Tierney 1979). When faculty do participate in policy decisions, such participation is fluid and situational (Baldridge et al. 1978). They move in and out of the decision process, rarely spending much time on a given issue. Fragmentation of faculty and administrators into interest groups with different goals and values culminates in conflict, which focuses the attention of professional staff on intraorganizational problems rather than on organization-environment relationships.

Organizations characterized by a high degree of insulation and fragmentation among staff essentially must forge agreements with broad factions inside and outside the college in the pursuit of goals and the production of outputs. These factions may have common or competing interests. Their impact is to magnify the effort required of administrators in representing multiple interests in the decision process and to call attention to the process of making decisions, not to the outcomes (Alfred 1987). To critics, this situation symbolizes the detachment of colleges and universities from the publics they serve. Institutions are best able to improve stature by matching programs and resources with opportunities, threats, and needs in the environment (Cope 1981; Hearn and Heydinger 1985; Thomas 1980). Excessive attention to issues of internal governance insulates the college from its environment, thus limiting opportunities to enhance stature.

Performance Attributes

Even if colleges and universities were organized to encourage rationality and flexibility in relationships between the institution and its environment, formidable problems would stand as obstacles to enhancing stature. Researchers and practitioners alike acknowledge the complexity, diffuseness, and ambiguity that typify educational goals and outcomes. Some have suggested that without meaningful and measurable objectives, it is impossible to assess the effectiveness of higher education (Chickering 1981). The problem with studying performance in colleges and universities lies in the fact that they are loosely coupled organizations without a core group of performance criteria that are relevant to organizational members, applicable across subunits, and comparable across institutions (Cameron 1978).

To understand the impact of inadequate performance criteria on institutional stature, it is necessary to recognize what stands

in the way and how public opinion might improve through assessing performance. Four obstacles stand in the way of measuring performance in colleges and universities:

1. Lack of visible commitment. *Most colleges and universities, particularly in the public sector, are multipurpose enterprises. Research, graduate instruction, and public service compete with undergraduate teaching for attention from faculty and administrators alike. And in the absence of incentives to the contrary, faculty follow the demands of their disciplines and training in approaching these tasks. Moreover, many institutions [that] concentrate exclusively on undergraduate teaching, especially community colleges, are characterized by considerable internal diversity in both clientele and in instructional goals. This diversity is contrasted with blandness of the majority of college and university mission statements and of most other public pronouncements of what the institution is about. Such statements are remarkable more for their sameness than their distinctiveness and give little symbolic focus for collective action.*

2. Fragmented responsibility. *A second major obstacle to performance measurement is the fragmented nature of responsibility for student success. For the most part, the effectiveness of undergraduate instruction, particularly in general education, is everybody's business but nobody's explicit responsibility. Considerable division of labor with respect to student development generally means that different individuals or offices are charged with dealing with particular "pieces" of students. There is generally no single place in the institution [that] can monitor or be held accountable for undergraduate performance as a whole.*

3. Lack of incentives for improvement. *Reinforcing organizational fragmentation is the lack of concrete reward for improvement. In the public sector, institutional budgets remain largely formula driven—a practice [that] encourages quantity production rather than allowing quality improvement. Within institutions, the constraints of formula budgeting are apparent in enrollment-based reallocation strategies and in the clear signals given to deans and faculty that the achievement of high numbers is important.*

These tendencies are magnified at most private institutions at which planning is largely tuition driven.

4. Lack of acceptable information about outcomes attained. *A major reason for lack of incentives is that there is little agreement about the basis on which they might be constructed. A root cause is the perception that instructional effectiveness as defined in terms of actual outcomes is difficult to measure. Many difficulties underlie this central theme. The first is purely cultural. Many of the presumed outcomes of higher education are held to be in principle unmeasurable, and attempts to assess them are resisted purely on this basis. A second problem is disagreement on what to measure. The intended outcomes of higher education are magnificently diverse and vary markedly across institutions of different type. Furthermore, different external constituencies have their own agendas about which outcomes should be assessed and consequently rewarded. A third problem is the fact that data on educational development are more complex than other kinds of managerial data. Because such data are collected indirectly through measurement instruments rather than. . .directly [through observation] and because the technology of measurement often involves the use of techniques [that] are not immediately "face valid" to policy makers, the difficulties of communicating their implications are considerable. Most institutional and state leaders would rather make decisions on something they understand. Finally, information on educational outcomes rarely directly tells institutional leaders what action to take. Unlike the kinds of numbers that managers are used to working with, it is difficult to link a particular outcome with a particular institutional policy or program that needs changing. Such data more often highlight the presence of a problem, provide a context for a decision, or serve as a stimulant for discussion* (Ewell 1987, pp. 26–27).

These obstacles combine in complex ways to prevent institutions from devoting systematic attention to assessment of performance. They also demonstrate the difficulty that colleges have in developing uniform definitions of effective performance and in collecting information that can be used to document effectiveness to the general public, states, and other funding sources. For example, lacking information about the relationship between costs and benefits, is it possible for presidents to say that effective performance is a function of the amount and type of financial resources available to the college? Can they say that performance will elevate when selective admissions and retention standards are employed that certify student input? Is effective performance a correlate of the academic credentials and experience of faculty that certify students' output following college attendance? Unfortunately, none of these performance criteria are adequate. Resources can be substantial but ineffectively or inefficiently allocated. Students may be highly qualified but grow and develop little during college. Faculty may possess superb academic credentials but employ outdated approaches to instruction. Simply put, no uniform definitions exist for effective performance in colleges and universities, nor has a consensus been reached about how it should be measured.

Finally, even if colleges had the resources and information technology to measure performance, doubts would exist as to their capacity to represent performance in meaningful ways to the public. Communication is deemed effective when a consumer receives information that fits a need or expectation. Consumer expectations (and needs) applied to postsecondary education are dualistic in nature, however. College and university administrators are finding that individuals and groups—legislators, business and industry officials, educational coordinating boards, state agencies—maintain multiple vantage points on the same issue, depending on the context in which the issue is viewed (Alfred 1987). Issues and events are becoming more complex. The number of ways in which they can be viewed—and the number of constituencies viewing them—has increased. In some cases, coalitions may develop among constituencies where none existed before. Coalition interests may merge on a particular issue, in response to a particular event, or in relationship to a specific outcome, even though their stated positions would indicate otherwise (Alfred 1987).

Conclusion
Attributes of academic organization and performance may limit the capacity of institutions to assess and enhance stature through responsiveness to public needs and expectations, especially in an era of changing accountability, expanded access to

information, and complex issues. Certain attributes of the academic organization may influence institutional responsiveness to external forces by delimiting domains of activity pursued by faculty and administrators. One attribute—the loosely coupled organization—may constrain the development of new programs and services by insulating faculty and administrators from external events and perspectives. Fluid and situational participation by faculty in decision making based on membership in a group may engender conflict that focuses attention on intraorganizational problems rather than on relationships between the organization and its environment.

A second attribute—ambiguous institutional goals and unclear performance objectives—may influence institution-environment relationships by rendering colleges ineffective in building positive relationships with constituencies. Current strategies for communication may not be sufficient to overcome this problem because they fail to account for differential values assigned to educational issues, events, and outcomes by multiple constituencies.

PRACTICES TO ENHANCE STATURE IN COMPLEX ORGANIZATIONS

As demonstrated in the previous section, colleges and universities differ sharply from other complex organizations in certain characteristics. All organizations have certain attributes in common, however (Weissman 1987). By nature, higher education institutions and other complex organizations are open systems, dependent on their environments (Katz and Kahn 1978). All must make decisions about economic resources, allocating scarce resources among competing priorities; all operate through an organization, getting tasks done through people; and all are affected by a changing environment (Doyle and New-bould 1980; Wasem 1978).

Every organization must perform a financial function insofar as money must be raised, managed, and budgeted according to sound business principles. Every organization must perform a production function in that it must conceive of the best way of arranging inputs to produce the outputs of the organization. Every organization must perform a personnel function in that people must be hired, trained, assigned, and promoted in the course of the organization's work. Every organization must perform a purchasing function in that it must acquire materials in an efficient way through comparing and selecting sources of supply. When we come to the marketing function, it is also clear that every organization performs marketing-like activities (Kotler and Levy 1978, p. 4).

Stature elevates over time as these organizations consistently deliver quality products and services to consumers and do so in a fashion that communicates distinctive patterns of organizational behavior in relationships with clients.

This section examines the strategies and practices to enhance stature in complex organizations. Colleges and universities seeking to improve their understanding of stature and how it develops may profit from the experience of other complex organizations. Business and industry, health care organizations, labor unions, and government agencies—all maintain continuing interest in the advancement of organizational prestige with product and service markets. Although practices to enhance stature used in for-profit organizations may have only a tenuous relationship to higher education institutions, several important questions must be asked. What techniques can colleges and universities borrow from for-profit and from nonprofit organizations to enhance stature? What practical steps can administra-

Louise Hessenflow, Sandy Whitesell, and Carolyn Kelley assisted in the review and synthesis of information presented in this section.

tors take to initiate efforts toward enhancing stature? The issue is one of generalizing to colleges and universities, given different goals, administrative structures, and funding sources.

For-profit Organizations

Enhancing stature in for-profit organizations, such as business and industry, involves the development of a comprehensive, realistic understanding of the product environment, the provision of products and services that reflect corporate sensitivity to consumers' needs, and a management organization that projects certain desirable attributes (for example, financial durability, innovation, selection and retention of quality staff). Stature elevates over time as these organizations consistently deliver quality products and services to consumers and do so in a fashion that communicates distinctive patterns of organizational behavior in relationships with clients.

Business and industry

Business and industrial organizations today are more competitive than they have been in decades. Deregulation of trucking, airlines, and a host of businesses has put the emphasis on survival. The breakup of the Bell System, the search for alternative sources of oil and energy, federal spending priorities, the revolutions in computers, health care, telecommunications, and banking have all put new demands on public- and private-sector organizations for corporate investment. A synthesis of the literature in trade and professional journals (*Fortune, Business Week, Forbes, Inc., Harvard Business Review*) describing characteristics and practices employed by successful organizations reveals 10 key attributes that underlie stature:

- Visibility of products and services
- Innovativeness
- Ability to attract, develop, and keep talent
- Quality of management
- Quality of products and services
- Management's responsiveness to crises
- Timeliness of strategic decisions
- Distinctiveness of operations
- Community and environmental responsibility
- Financial soundness and durability.

In looking at a corporation, the public is inclined to link the reputation of a company with the *visibility of its products and services*, which includes factors like the company's acronym and trademark, market research, marketing and packaging, product appearance, association, and progress advertising. Most corporations use acronyms and trademarks to communicate a specific image (Strenski 1984). For example, a commercial bank might employ a design and colors on its logo to reflect a message of security, integrity, and financial soundness (Diefenbach 1983). Similarly, product appearance identifies a company with a discernible image. Between 1980 and 1985, the Howard Johnson Company counted on its traditional, middle American market to fill hotel rooms and restaurants out of a sense of loyalty, irrespective of the condition of its products and services (*Business Week* 1985). Since 1980, however, the company had developed a reputation for bland, overpriced food and shoddy accommodations; earnings were flat, and room occupancy declined to 63 percent. In 1985, the corporation found itself needing to spend $700 million for a new chain of hotels, plus an additional $78 million to refurbish existing hotels.

Market research, packaging, manipulation of events and situations to create platforms to enhance image, progress advertising, and imaging through association contribute to the public's recognition and confidence in corporate products and services. Market research on consumers' attitudes toward corporate products and services and a broad range of confidence issues is a common practice in business and industry (Mitchell 1983). The 1983 experience of the McNeil Corporation with Tylenol provides an excellent example of the value of market research in enhancing stature.

In 1967, the McNeil Corporation introduced Tylenol, a new nonaspirin pain reliever, to the consumer drug market. In the 1970s, the product line was expanded to include both tablet and capsule forms. By September 1982, Tylenol had cornered over 37 percent of the pain reliever market (*New York Times* 17 September 1983), and McNeil executives were confident Tylenol would take over 50 percent of the market by 1986 (*Fortune* 29 November 1982, p. 45). In late September 1982, however, the first of seven people died in the Chicago area after taking extra-strength Tylenol capsules that had been laced with cyanide. As the tragedy struck, consumers' confidence in the Tylenol product vanished, and by November, Tylenol's share of the market had dropped to 7 percent. Market analysts predicted that Tylenol would never regain its market share and that the product line would eventually be forced out of the market (*New York Times* 17 September 1983).

Believing they had a good product, the makers of Tylenol implemented a marketing strategy to regain its share of the market. An aggressive market research program produced some startling findings: A large majority of people were aware that Tylenol had been involved with the poisoning, believed that Tylenol was not responsible for the deaths, were hesitant to buy Tylenol in the future, and would come back to the product if they had been frequent users (*Fortune* 29 November 1982). A strategic plan was prepared to recapture frequent users, which involved repackaging the product in safety-sealed caplets, persuading health care providers to begin recommending Tylenol to patients, distributing discount coupons, giving discounts to retailers, and replacing Tylenol discarded during the scare at no cost (Powell 1986). Finally, a new advertising campaign was started, emphasizing the trust—both past and present—that customers had in McNeil products. The strategy worked. By enhancing the product's visibility and the public's trust, the company regained its 30 percent market share in less than one year.

Product visibility does not guarantee future profits and reputational success for business and industry. Faced with changing market forces, corporations are using creative marketing and packaging to create new images for old products by changing the corporate name—Exxon (formerly Esso) and Navistar (International Harvester), for example—and replacing the corporate symbol (National Broadcasting Corporation) to cultivate a modern, high-tech image for traditional products. Similarly, a growing number of companies are employing strategies like association and progress advertising to heighten consumers' recognition and confidence in corporate products and services. Employing the concept of association, Leader Federal Bank in Memphis, Tennessee, enhanced the visibility of its services by acting as a "credit enhancer" for a tax-exempt bond issue that enabled the city to fund construction of a large apartment complex (Spooner 1985). First Federal Savings Bank in Cleveland, Ohio, sponsors a continuous series of advertisements designed to inform depositors and the general public about the condition of the institution and its progress in specific spheres of activity (Spooner 1985).

A 1985 *Fortune* survey of 8,000 business executives, directors, and financial analysts showed *capacity for innovation* to be an element critical to success in high-performance corporations like 3M, Rubbermaid, and Procter and Gamble (Hutton 1986). Three-M has established a plan to generate at least 25 percent of sales each year from products introduced in the previous five years. Part and parcel of an environment that encourages experimentation and risk, innovation at 3M is perhaps the key building block of stature with the general public. Rubbermaid has introduced more than 500 new products in the past five years, and Procter and Gamble has entered a number of new product categories. Both companies attempt to build stature through providing products to the public either in anticipation of emerging needs or in response to expressed needs. Innovative corporations operate in accord with a principle of linkage between social needs and the character of the organization and its employees. These organizations base decisions about product development, marketing, and withdrawal on the attitudes and expectations of the public, trying to fit decisions about products with what the consumer would "expect the organization to do." They undertake intensive strategic analysis, evaluate performance continually and unsentimentally, and discard money-losing operations in favor of experimental products with new markets (Hutton 1986).

A third attribute of stature in business and industrial organizations is the capacity to *attract, develop, and keep talent*. Highly visible corporations like Exxon and Procter and Gamble promote from within to attract, hold, and develop commitment in talented employees (Hutton 1986). Recruiting is conducted on college campuses on a discipline-by-discipline basis, and career employment is encouraged. Executive development is performed systematically through cross-training personnel in different company divisions.

Studies of corporate reputation conducted by *Fortune* point to the *quality of management* and the *quality of products and services* as important attributes in judging corporate stature. Corporate style—the integrity and perceived expertise of officers, acts of friendliness by front-line staff, the attractiveness and orderliness of facilities, and the image established for a company through presentations by officers—contributes to consumers' confidence in a company's products and services (Stancill 1984). Corporate executives making "folksy" and disorganized presentations for prime contracts or underbidding the competition by one-half or even two-thirds for large projects undermine confidence in the company. Companies like the

Chrysler Corporation and National Steel provide executives with training in public communications to improve media skills (Shell 1982). Some companies (Continental Airlines, Kroger Company, and Johnson & Johnson) have acquired and examined public opinion data related to consumers' interests, attitudes toward labor, and confidence in social institutions to determine adjustments in management philosophy required to build or restore consumer confidence (Saporito 1983). Executives of Continental Airlines sought to change Continental's image from an airline with financial and management problems to one with major union problems as a method to marshal public support and confidence in the airline (Pauly et al. 1986). Timberland, Inc., abandoning 20 years of practice as a family-operated business making quality, lower-priced boots, restructured its approach to management to include the use of public opinion data and public relations programming to transform a utility product into a fashion item (Rhodes 1982). It increased prices to equate cost with quality, purchased advertising space in upscale magazines, and sought big-name stores to merchandise its product. Between 1973 and 1979, company sales grew to $16 million as a small, family-owned company—through transformation in management and public recognition of product quality—converted a regional business into a national business with a comprehensive market (Rhodes 1982).

Corporate responsiveness to crises implicit in management's efforts to improve or protect corporate image under emergency conditions is a rapidly emerging attribute of stature in for-profit organizations. Corporations can favorably or unfavorably position themselves in a competitive market by their reaction to crises like product tampering, natural disasters, and equipment failure. Recent examples of the role that management can play in improving or diminishing corporate stature in crises include the Tylenol crisis, tampering with Gerber baby food, tampering with Hygrade products, the Union Carbide disaster in Bhopal, and the safety setbacks for Delta Airlines. In three cases, officials at McNeil, Union Carbide, and Delta Airlines significantly enhanced the stature of their companies through the management techniques they used to handle the crises. Communication with the public was straightforward regarding the gravity of the situation, information was released on a timely basis in response to requests from external groups, the number of individuals providing information was limited, and centralized channels of communication were used to release information (Mitchell 1983). Delta Airlines restored consumers' confidence in the airline through a series of internal and external audits. Following a rash of incidents that tarnished the airline's record of safety and service, corporate officials appointed a committee of pilots to conduct an extensive internal investigation of operating procedures and a safety review panel to analyze the series of incidents imperiling the airline's reputation (Johnson and Smith 1987).

In a 1984 survey of nearly 400 companies with less than $500 million in sales, Western Union Corporation found that 47 percent had crisis communications plans (Couretas 1985). For-profit corporations are initiating efforts to scrutinize their entire base of operations for susceptibility to all types of crises, including erosion of the public's confidence in management and product quality. They conduct simulations of major crises through crisis management units to upgrade procedures and to protect corporate stature with the public (Mitroff 1986). More important, the crisis management units serve as the conscience of the organization, raising the questions that most executives prefer not to consider: How vulnerable is the corporation to changing public opinion induced by vacillation in the economy, demographic transition, and social movements? The function of a crisis management unit is to continually prepare an organization for the potential occurrence of every act to diminish stature that can be envisioned.

Corporations that enhance stature through aligning company products and services with consumers' needs make *timely strategic decisions* and have the capacity to *demonstrate distinctive operations*. Martin Marietta Corporation emerged from its takeover battle with Bendix Corporation in 1983 a much healthier company because it had learned to make hard decisions quickly about strategic facets of its corporate structure and operations (Chakravoty 1985). Saddled with a poor debt/equity ratio and burgeoning problems with investors and shareholders, Martin Marietta sold less productive operations and returned to its earlier status as a devoted supplier to large customers. At the same time, it decided to further its involvement in high-technology guidance systems, data systems, and communications, thus positioning the company to enter the competition for long-term defense contracts and to diminish the earnings volatility of its operations. Investors' confidence and earnings improved dramatically after what had begun as a takeover bid for a bloated corporation resulted in a streamlined operation capable of making rapid decisions about its future based on solid strategic information (Chakravoty 1985).

Pepsico Corporation, confronted with declining earnings in 1983 as a result of a scandal in its overseas operation, weakening currencies, and the loss of talented top managers, moved quickly to restore consumers' confidence by calling attention to the distinctiveness of its operations through new product lines, periodic renewal of old product lines, and innovative contractual strategies with retailers that guaranteed profit margins of total sales if Pepsico products were provided additional shelf space (Fisher 1983).

A characteristic shared by many corporations viewed favorably by consumers and investors is the capacity to champion the consumer through the exercise of *community and environmental responsibility* and demonstrated expertise in communications. Companies that assign meaning to the concept of "corporate social responsibility" develop the capacity to shape consumers' preferences rather than simply to react to emerging interests. They actively anticipate consumers' needs and develop action programs to respond to them. In the 1970s, when oil companies were under attack from environmental groups, Atlantic Richfield Corporation financed a Sierra Club study of the impact of the Alaska oil pipeline on caribou migrations (Nulty 1985). The chairman of Union Carbide Corporation traveled to Bhopal, India, in 1984 to personally direct the efforts of the company toward preservation of public safety when toxic fumes leaked from a regional plant (Sasseen 1985). Waste Management Incorporated in Illinois, rocked by a full-page article in the *New York Times* detailing the company's illegal disposal and waste storage procedures, hired an independent legal investigator to assess the short-term problem (Behar 1985). To address long-term problems about its image with consumers and investors, the company created an environmental compliance program—a department of in-house auditors reporting directly to company headquarters—and initiated a series of television commercials showing steps taken to ensure public safety.

Corporations that condition employees to think of the organization as a consumer company promote stature through a relationship of public service with consumers. Consumers see and understand company officials who possess the technology to develop needed products, which may induce public service as diverse as running for office, giving speeches at Rotary lunches, or sponsoring community events (Hutton 1986).

For-profit corporations are always vulnerable to changing public perceptions of their products and services. Certain corporations—AT&T, Exxon, IBM, Coca-Cola, Boeing, Dow Jones, Merck, and 3M—maintain steady relationships with consumers and investors because of a continuing aura of *financial soundness and durability* (Hutton 1986). Such companies can afford to make mistakes (Coca-Cola's discontinuing its traditional product in favor of a product made with a new formula, for example) and still maintain stature through a traditional reputation for financial soundness. Moreover, financially sound corporations maintain the capacity to "bleed profusely and survive" (Hutton 1986), providing the foundation necessary for innovation and risky ventures. They can afford to market new products and services and to withdraw them quickly if they fail. Profits provide the surest path to respect. The 10 most advanced corporations in the United States, according to a 1984 *Fortune* survey, showed a median return on shareholders' equity of 20 percent, compared to 13.5 percent for all Fortune 500 companies. None of the 10 companies have had an annual loss in over 35 years, thus adding to their stature as trusted organizations worthy of consumers' and investors' support (Hutton 1986).

Health care organizations

The 1980s have seen enormous change in the design and delivery of health care. Complex technology, the challenge of intensifying competition, rising costs, increasingly resistant third-party payers, the wellness movement, and the health-involved consumer are but a few of the major forces that have coalesced to reposition health care. Quickly eroding is the consumer's sacrosanct view of the physician and the hospital that historically have controlled decisions about health care. Health care is now delivered in an environment in which consumers are exercising choice among alternatives and a participative role in decisions.

Marketing and public relations are becoming a cornerstone of efforts to maintain and improve stature with the public. Hospitals attempting to set themselves apart from the competition spent $80 million in 1985 on advertising designed to demonstrate distinctive patient care facilities and services (*Ann Arbor News* 30 June 1985). The health care industry uses some of the following techniques to enhance stature:

1. *Public relations*. Establishing and maintaining favorable images in the minds of those requiring access to health care services.
2. *Managing price sensitivities*. Coordinating price levels and how costs are paid, and managing the psychic costs experienced by consumers of health care services.
3. *Distribution strategies*. Analyzing the proximity of clients to health care facilities and the needs of clients for specific services. Such analyses are an important dimension of decisions made about the distribution of health services (the location of services and transportation arteries, for example).
4. *Communications*. Using advertising, personal communications, and publicity through various media.
5. *Countering the competition*. Engaging strategies to change or reinforce public attitudes toward the use of particular services that are marketed as having special or superior attributes.
6. *Neutralizing the costs of new services*. Undertaking research to determine the anticipated costs associated with new organizational services and whether such services outweigh the benefits individuals anticipate receiving (Hessenflow 1985).

Intense competition for patients and escalating public concern about the costs of health care have resulted in special pricing programs for health services. Some hospitals, for example, have created a "Special Delivery" package for prenatal care and birth. The package includes prenatal care in the obstetrics clinic, labor and delivery charges, a 24- to 36-hour hospital stay, and a follow-up medical visit for mother and infant (*Ann Arbor News* 30 June 1985). Hospitals are undertaking significant efforts to avoid price-driven marketing strategies in favor of strategies that emphasize special services, care, and treatment of patients.

Practically all hospitals, particularly those in urban regions engaged in intense competition, use marketing strategies designed to favorably influence public opinion by matching health care services with consumers' attributes and needs. For these organizations, "stature" is a process of selection influenced by three exogenous variables: (1) the background characteristics of the consumer, (2) the shared perceptions of "health" between the health care organization and the consumer, and (3) the community's social structure and patterns of information flow (Hessenflow 1985). Information about specific attributes of consumers (the "propensity to assume risk" or the nature of "control beliefs," for example) is examined as part of decision making about the organization, delivery, and marketing of health services. To illustrate, some hospitals have established decision support systems to provide information about the effects of past experience, certain attitudinal states (optimism, pessimism, or fatalism), and actions on consumers' propensity to assume risk in health care decisions (Hessenflow 1985). Similarly, the effects of certain variables, such as place of residence and level of educational attainment on an individual's general feeling of being able to influence aspects of the environment, have been examined using information systems. Armed with this information, health organizations have been able to maintain or enhance stature by aligning services with consumers' attributes and needs.

Not-for-profit Organizations
Professional associations
Given the ever-changing nature of professional and staff roles in complex organizations, the development of stature is a paramount concern to professional associations supporting these organizations. Nursing and medicine are professions undergoing change in which associations have assumed responsibility for interpreting consumers' needs to the profession and professional services to the consumer.

The nursing profession is the nation's second largest profession and plays a critical and expanding role in all phases of health care delivery. While most professionals work to capitalize on media methods—television in particular—professional nursing faces the distinct dilemma of attempting to dismantle and restructure an image created by the media to a stature more befitting a health profession. Researchers have documented a negative and unrealistic image of nurses publicized by the media between 1950 and 1980 that includes altruistic motivations for entering nursing, performance primarily in a support role to other health professionals, the lack of problem-solving, evaluation, and administrative skills, being remiss in providing basic physical, comforting measures, and not engaging in expanded roles, such as patient education and scholarly endeavors (Kalisch and Kalisch 1983). Two researchers with a sociological background illuminate perceptions held by the public of nurses and enlighten understanding of how stature forms in the professions (Berger and Luckmann 1966). They argue that knowledge concerns itself more with "common sense than theoretical abstractions." Individuals seek some type of orderly, structured, physical, cognitive, and emotional milieu. Accordingly, people create a reality for themselves about ideas, which includes nursing or any other phenomenon, that is based on things individuals "know." The cultural lag implicit in current public knowledge about professions will continue to exist until it is directly challenged by new knowledge (Berger and Luckmann 1966). This principle makes up the focal point of efforts to enhance the stature of nursing. Strategies for enhancement rest on a predominant, consistent set of knowledge, ideas, and beliefs about nursing that yield an ideal or consonant image for the public (Kalisch and Kalisch 1980). The absence of consistency and the ensuing internal contradiction provide a cognitively dissonant image of nursing that results in a tendency to reduce dissonance by changing attitudes and beliefs. Such changes are not necessarily grounded in reality.

Accordingly, nursing professional associations have organized a comprehensive "media watch" program involving the monitoring of media along critical parameters that shape the desired or undesired view of nursing (Kalisch, Kalisch, and Clinton 1982). These parameters include variables such as humanism, scholarship, achievement, sex object, career orientation and motivation, professional competence, education, and administrative ability. The monitoring process is coupled with:

- The building of strong media contacts
- Education of media executives and personnel about a more realistic view of nursing
- Conferences that bring nurses and media professionals together to examine strategies for more effective image building in nursing
- Media consultation, particularly in the area of script writing
- Awards and prizes in recognition of positive media depictions of nurses and nursing
- Health information columns and programs on local stations to reach the public with positive impressions
- The development of literature about careers in nursing

- News coverage of real-life events about nursing
- Personal and phone contacts before and after submitting news releases to increase the likelihood that a story will be printed and to enhance the chances that the story will communicate a positive image of nursing
- Extensive press packages with adequate information for reporters
- The facilitation of media relations with reporters to ensure that good, adequate information is provided (Hessenflow 1985).

Strategies for enhancement cannot compensate for inherently weak products and services.

Practices to enhance stature employed in medicine are best summarized in a 1984 American Medical Association report to its Board of Trustees, "AMA Activities Related to the Public Image of Physicians" (Coury 1984), which stresses the need to increase efforts to measure the public's expectations for and satisfaction with medical practice and physicians' use of the information so as to better serve their patients. In addition, the report reaffirms emphasis on the collection and analysis of information on issues that affect the public's perception of physicians. These statements underscore the importance AMA attaches to the public image of physicians.

The AMA has closely monitored public opinion on several dimensions of physicians' image. Generally speaking, public perceptions remain positive in areas such as the availability of care, knowledge of medicine and science, and dedication and humility. Perceptions become more negative with respect to other issues, however: fees and income, the ability of patients to talk with their physicians, and access to care among the poor and elderly (Hessenflow 1985). The most negative opinions center on the reasonableness of physicians' fees and the amount of time spent with patients (Hessenflow 1985).

To counter negative public perceptions and to improve stature, the AMA is employing a wide range of activities to improve the public image of physicians. Most of them are centered on eliminating or managing informational gaps regarding health practices. Among the specific strategies employed are a consumer book series on public health issues, science news for radio and television, public service announcements, media tours for the president of the AMA to address business and civic groups, and cable network television programs (Coury 1984). A second category of strategies relates to health promotion and primary prevention, including programs that attempt to reduce violence on television, increase rates of immunization, improve safety in sports, reduce alcohol abuse, and educate youths to the dangers of smoking and sex, and sponsorship of fitness events that link, in the mind of the public, the scientific knowledge of physicians with a visible intent to help individuals improve personal fitness and health (Coury 1984). A third category of strategies relates to public image programs targeted to medical students and young physicians during their education and training. Designed to assist physicians to cope with widely held public perceptions about routine practice problems, such as long waiting times and lack of time devoted to discussion between patient and physician, strategies recognize that organizational efforts to improve the image of physicians are inherently limited and can never replace the actions of individual physicians committing themselves to spending more time with patients, giving them better service, and discussing their fees (Coury 1984). This approach underscores the idea that the pathway to improving stature is centered in the quality of programs and services. Strategies for enhancement cannot compensate for inherently weak products and services.

Government agencies

In 1974, the U.S. Department of Defense turned to an all-volunteer force. In the first two years the project appeared headed toward failure: Throughout the mid-1970s, the Army found it difficult to fill its ranks, and by the late 1970s, nearly half of the volunteers were drawn from the lowest acceptable mental categories (*Washington Post* 10 December 1984). A 1974 report stated that "the preliminary information available indicated that the all-volunteer approach is not working well and may finally result in the military services having to greatly decrease either the size or the overall quality of the force" (*Congressional Quarterly Almanac* 1973, p. 168).

The disappointing numbers of volunteers stepping forward was not the result of a lack of effort by government recruiters to attract new members. In FY 1971, 13,000 persons were employed in recruiting activities, and by FY 1974, the number had grown to 32,000 (*Congressional Quarterly Almanac* 1973, p. 168). Although the Army had been advertising for many years, it had never conducted extensive market research. After evaluating a complex series of attitude studies and survey groups, the Army decided it had a problem with stature because it was viewed as stodgy and pedestrian, especially when contrasted with the high-technology, modern-skills image projected by the other services (*Washington Post* 9 December 1984). The highly successful "Be All You Can Be" campaign began in January 1981, after a year of development (*Washington Post* 9 December 1984). The new campaign was a great success. By 1982, enlistments were up to 103 percent of targets (*New York Times* 13 October 1982). In addition, the new enlistments were the highest-quality recruits the Army had ever seen, with 93 percent of them having graduated from high school, contrasted with a 1980 enlistment group that included 50 percent of its recruits from the lowest acceptable mental aptitude category, those with reading skills below the ninth grade level (*Wall Street Journal* 21 August 1984).

Through serial commercials—a single ad was not useful because the message to be conveyed was complex—the Army upgraded its image from stodgy and pedestrian to glamorous and high tech. Using the marketing tactics of Coca-Cola and Allstate Insurance, the Army successfully combined the allure of high technology with the promise of socioeconomic mobility (through advanced technical training) to enhance its stature in the eyes of youth requiring economic and financial security in a technological society.

State and local government agencies have experienced similar problems of image. As part of their quest for public support of building and construction programs, regional products, and spending through tourism, government agencies are implementing novel programs for matching public needs with regional resources. Public relations and urban planning experts are hired to promote public construction projects on the behalf of state government agencies, community education and legislative awareness programs are formulated to promote a positive image for state projects, and test market advertising strategies are employed to gauge the effect of product promotion (*Ann Arbor News* 19 May 1985).

Some government agencies have experienced improved stature as a result of executives' leadership style and visibility. For example, staff morale and the public image of the Federal Bureau of Investigation was at a low ebb in 1978 following J. Edgar Hoover's iron-fisted tenure, the Watergate scandal, and the short tenure of directors as a result of civil rights violations. Its highly favorable Gallup rating of 87 percent in 1965 had dropped to 37 percent in 1975. With the appointment of a new director (William Webster) in 1978, public opinion began to change (*Ann Arbor News* 14 April 1986). Combining open and direct communication, candor, and concern about personal credibility with tactical decision making that refocused the FBI's investigative strategy on criminal activity, not dissent, Webster was able to restore public credibility for the FBI. The evidence of success was implicit in quantitative information filtered to the media in 1986: the indictment or conviction of 20 Mafia bosses between 1979 and 1984, the arrest of 11 spies in 1985 compared to only three in 1978, and decline in the number of cases involving corruption of agents (*Ann Arbor News* 14 April 1986).

Labor unions

For many years, labor unions focused on management as the target of efforts to win concessions for workers and to maintain harmony and a solid image within their ranks. Following a prolonged period of recession in key industries and the battering of technological change, foreign competition, damaging regulatory decisions, management's union-breaking strategies, and the disbanding of the air traffic controllers union (PATCO) by President Reagan in 1981, the unions discovered the need to build a positive public image. Consequently, labor unions have recently turned to advertising to convey their mission to the public. They have employed five basic approaches to improve stature with the public: beginning a multimillion dollar television advertising and programming campaign, stressing the cooperation of unions and management through concessions in salary and benefits, seating union members on corporate boards, acquiring partial ownership of companies (and owner responsibilities) through stock purchases, and publicly advocating specific issues to convey to the public what unions stand for.

Principles for Application to Colleges and Universities

College and university administrators who are interested in stature should know that 14 basic, important principles can be extracted from business and industry and selectively applied to higher education (see table 5).

TABLE 5
PRINCIPLES TO ENHANCE STATURE IN COMPLEX ORGANIZATIONS

Principle	Organizational Practice	Example	Effectiveness Indicator(s)
Product visibility	• Simplified reporting of organizational operations and performance to improve corporate visibility with clients	Exxon Corporation	Improved public recognition of corporate products measured in increased sales
	• Progress advertising with a focus on results (outcomes), not operations, to improve product visibility	Leader Federal Bank (Tennessee) First Federal Savings (Ohio)	Increased public awareness of corporate performance measured through opinion surveys and frequency of mention in media
	• Market research to match organizational products with clients' needs	Saxony Ice Company	Increased sales
Continuous assessment of performance	• Systematic research on product performance (sales, consumers' satisfaction, competitors' performance, etc.) to determine product strengths, weaknesses, and needs for improvement	McNeil Corporation	Favorable public opinion toward company products measured in increased sales
Management of cost sensitivity	• Evaluation and management of cost levels through research on the "psychic cost" to the public (cost levels at which public perceptions of price exceed those of benefits) of products and services	Urban and suburban hospitals	Favorable public perceptions of the relationship between benefits and costs in delivery of health services
	• Continuous monitoring and updating of information about product quality and value to overcome lag in public knowledge	Nursing profession	Change in public attitudes toward the nursing profession to reflect modern ideas about profession

TABLE 5 (continued)

Capacity for innovation	• Willingness to take risks in the development of new products and services, pricing strategies, and marketing techniques based on information about consumers' needs and preferences	Rubbermaid Corporation 3M Corporation Procter and Gamble	Number of new products entering the market over a specified period of time
	• Special packaging and pricing of products and services to attract clients	St. Joseph Hospital (Flint, Michigan)	Increased use of services by clients
Response to pressure situations	• Development of a crisis plan to manage emergency situations involving organizational products and services	Union Carbide Delta Airlines	Existence of a "crisis plan," including strategies for effective communication with the public
Timely strategic decisions	• Hard decisions about strategic operations (product termination, introduction, diversification, and pricing) to enhance performance, stave off competition, or protect organizational interests and integrity	Martin Marietta Corporation	Stable or increased sales; continuation of organizational autonomy in management and operations
Distinctiveness in products, services, and operations	• Products, services, and operations that establish organizational stature with the public because they are one of a kind, superior to competitors, or unparalleled in quality and cost	Pepsico Corporation	Increased sales associated with new and continuing products
	• Innovative marketing strategies that depict organizational products, services, and operations in a manner leading to a comparative advantage over competitors	Chrysler Corporation	Increased sales in relationship to competitors

Community and environmental responsibility	• Public service programming involving commitment of organizational resources (human and financial) to the solution of regional problems and issues	Atlantic Richfield Corporation	Favorable public opinion toward corporate management and products
Demonstrated expertise in communications	• Employees' orientation toward customer service developed through recruiting, hiring, orientation, and training; evaluation and reward systems; and identification of problems and solutions	Procter and Gamble	Increased sales
	• Monitoring of media to identify positive and negative stereotypes applied to organizational products, services, operations, and professional staff	Nursing profession	Favorable media treatment of organization or profession
	• Market research on consumers' needs, preferences, attitudes, values, and opinions to align product advertising with consumers' interests	Howard Johnson Corporation Timberland Corporation	Increased sales
	• Training programs for staff on how to relate to clients based on the assumption that the actions of individuals in one-on-one relationships (with clients) are most important	American Medical Association	Increased sales; favorable public perception of products and services
Persona and visibility of leader	• Special attention to the distinctive leadership characteristics and attributes of corporate executives through advertising and information released to the news media; making corporate success become synonymous with the profile of the CEO	Chrysler Corporation (Lee Iacocca)	Increased sales
		FBI (William Webster)	Expanded media interest in leader's products and services

TABLE 5 (continued)

Orientation toward client service	• Corporate practices and policies engendering rapid responsiveness to consumers' needs for product repair and replacement and new products, and guarantee of products' quality in relationship to consumers' needs and expectations	Chrysler Corporation	Increased sales
	• Provision of information to consumers describing the results of corporate tests of product quality and consumers' satisfaction with product cost and quality	McNeil Corporation	Increased sales; expressions of customers' satisfaction
Financial durability and soundness	• Publication of information in annual reports, marketing documents, news media, and advertisements demonstrating significant corporate profits, accumulation of assets, and investment capacity over an extended period of time	Dow Jones Coca-Cola Exxon	Constantly increasing sales
Traditional prestige	• Corporate reputation built on the basis of product and service visibility with the public over an extended period of time	IBM	Name recognition, public visibility, stable or increasing sales
Capacity to attract and hold talented staff	• Incentive and professional development programs that provide opportunities for staff mobility within the organization, thereby serving to attract and retain staff	Exxon IBM	Ability to attract top-quality staff Low staff turnover

Summary

In response to changing conditions in the economy, public opinion, and the behavior of competitors, for-profit and non-profit organizations have instituted a variety of techniques to enhance stature. Measured through sales volume, corporate visibility, and change in public opinion, most techniques have focused on improvement in corporate products and services based on information about consumers' needs, interests, values, and satisfactions. Significant resources have been spent on opinion research, marketing, improved client service, and staff development to improve the public's perception of organizational products and operations.

Although stature has become a topic of significant interest to colleges and universities, understanding is limited as to how it forms, how it can be measured and improved, and the extent to which principles borrowed from other types of organizations can be applied to higher education. This section has demonstrated that certain principles can be suggested to college and university administrators and considered for application. Among the most important of these principles are those concerned with (1) relating organizational products and services to consumers' needs, (2) allocating resources for improvement of organizational products and development of new products, (3) assessing the quality, appeal, and benefits of organizational products and services, and (4) advancing the organization's image with important constituencies. These principles can be examined in context with the working definition and model presented earlier and converted into guidelines to enhance stature in colleges and universities. Guidelines will not hold meaning for college faculty and administrators, however, in the absence of information about practices used by postsecondary institutions to enhance stature, which is the focus of the next section.

COLLEGE AND UNIVERSITY PRACTICES

The strategies employed by complex organizations to enhance stature focus on a very important fact: public- and private-sector organizations invest significant time and resources in activities designed to favorably influence public opinion. Throughout the higher education community, interest is burgeoning in stature, its antecedents, and its dynamics following a period of decline in public confidence in social institutions. Organizational charts are being altered to include public affairs staff with responsibility for advancement of institutional interests with multiple publics: state legislatures, federal agencies, foundations, alumni, private donors, and state government agencies. In a few scattered cases, vigorous efforts are being mounted to conduct research on public attitudes as a foundation for decisions about programs and resources (Lorenzo and Krnacik 1986).

Assessment of what colleges are doing and what they need to do to enhance stature is an important issue. We have so far referred to the fact that "stature" in colleges and universities is used interchangeably with concepts of "effectiveness" and "quality." The systems model presented earlier distinguishes stature from related concepts by conceptualizing it as the product of interaction among forces in the external environment and attributes of the academic organization. Attributes of the academic organization were viewed as an important dimension of stature because they condition the institution's response to the external environment. Through setting goals, planning, allocating resources, and marketing, faculty and administrators facilitate or impede the development of stature. The issue that remains to be addressed is exactly how colleges and universities build stature through specific strategies and techniques they employ with on- and off-campus groups.

With few exceptions, the literature has been dominated by descriptions of what colleges are doing to enhance quality through assessment; a different focus is evident, however, in the literature dealing with business, government, health care, and not-for-profit organizations. Among these organizations, the focus is on stature with the consumers of their products and services. The literature on complex organizations has focused on answering the question, "How well are organizational products and services perceived by the public?" The literature on

The literature until now has focused almost entirely on descriptions of institutions' achieving goals, and it has not developed prescriptions for assessment of stature.

Richard Bentley assisted in the review and synthesis of information presented in this section.

higher education has focused on other questions: "How well are institutions achieving their goals?" and "What are the organizational characteristics that lead to achieving goals?"

If the focus of the literature on higher education were to shift to another question—"What is the stature of colleges and universities based on public perception of programs, services, and resources?"—an important area of inquiry would come into being. That is, the literature until now has focused almost entirely on descriptions of institutions' achieving goals, and it has not developed prescriptions for assessment of stature. The literature that deals with stature generally is not empirically based, and it has centered almost exclusively on administrators' descriptions of effective techniques for improving the capacity of individual institutions to procure resources from specific constituencies—attracting more and better students, improving legislative appropriations, attracting support from donors, and maximizing the involvement of alumni in institutional campaigns. Unfortunately, administrators' descriptions have been criticized as being limited to the resource side of the institution and contributing little to the assessment of stature. The intent of the remaining sections, then, is to examine the literature on college and university stature to determine what institutions are doing and to prescribe actions that colleges will need to take in the future to improve stature.

What Colleges Are Doing to Enhance Stature

Examination of the literature on institutional advancement reveals that most institutions have attempted to enhance stature through short-term marketing practices designed to improve the position of the institution with multiple constituencies: prospective students, parents, alumni, state legislators, representatives from business and industry, congressional officials, and civic organizations. The customary practice has been to mold constituencies' perceptions through five methods, all of which are subject to direct control by the institution: (1) published materials describing educational programs, services, practices, and policies that demonstrate the institution's understanding of clients' needs and interests; (2) constituents' involvement in campus-based activities that improve understanding of institutional operations; (3) outreach activities that bring the campus directly to constituencies at times and locations dictated by convenience; (4) published assessment data describing the educational outcomes of students that improve the public's understanding of institutional performance; and (5) behavior of leaders that favorably influences public opinion.

Institutional information demonstrating sensitivity to clients' needs

Most, if not all, colleges and universities disseminate published information (catalogs, descriptive brochures, video information, and so on) describing institutional programs and services to prospective students in an effort to entice them into enrollment. Colleges also send an array of information to providers of resources (alumni, state legislators, private donors, business and industry, among others) to encourage public and private contributions. In a growing number of cases, the institution hires an advertising agency or marketing firm to assist in the development of institutional publications. The common practice is to describe why an institution is unique in terms of the programs and services it offers to different publics rather than the outcomes and cost versus benefits it renders based on research and assessment.

In their simplest form, institutional publications provide an image for the institution through the college emblem or logo. Colleges and universities nationwide have spent thousands of dollars to hire consultants to redesign logos and to trademark and copyright them. Administrators maintain that a distinctive logo developed through consumer research communicates important characteristics of the institution and builds visibility as it grows on the public.

Carried to an extreme, institutional publications can reflect almost total insensitivity to the needs of consumers and resource providers. Consider the example of the college attempting to explain complicated federal financial aid programs to potential students and their parents through brochures filled with technical language. Not only could such ill-conceived publications discourage favorable response, but by making the institution look detached and insensitive, they may be counterproductive. Additionally, they may undermine relations with potential sources of revenue, such as students and parents.

Colleges seeking to improve their stature through published information are beginning to forge closer bonds with external publics through information packaging and involvement strategies. For example, when Drew University updated the 1984 prospectus for its College of Liberal Arts, it started by obtaining ideas from faculty and students in group meetings and brainstorming sessions (Myers 1985). Reflecting on their interests and opinions, students made suggestions on the theme "50 well-known reasons to be at Drew and 50 little-known reasons to be at Drew." Many of the suggestions were incorporated into institutional publications marketing the college to prospective students and parents. When Connecticut College decided to publish individual profiles in its view book, students were asked for help in planning and producing the publication (Myers 1985). Students' involvement extended to visits with high school students to see what kind of information they would look for in a view book. At Mills College (California), students review proposed designs, evaluate photographs, and assist in the final selection of a design for marketing and recruiting literature (Myers 1985).

Colleges and universities turn to experts and media sources intuitively to improve visibility. Seeking a systematic and cost-effective way of gaining visibility through newspaper supplements, Pennsylvania State University initiated a procedure of targeting news features to newspaper special supplements (Jones 1984). A 1982 statewide survey of all daily newspapers revealed the papers that published special editions devoted to specific topics. College staff monitored copy deadlines, topics of special supplements, and institutional activities in an effort to maximize visibility. Surveys of public opinion improved the capacity of the university to match information describing program and service benefits with public interest. For example, the university was able to demonstrate the utility of campus research on child development by contributing four articles representing the views of professors in a special supplement on baby care published by the *Philadelphia Inquirer* (Jones 1984).

The news media are not the sole and primary focus of colleges and universities attempting to improve stature through client-sensitive information, however. Given the current emphasis on marketing and economic development, colleges are collaborating with state agencies, elected officials, and business and industry representatives in the design of information about regional business climates that will both assist existing business and attract new business (Bers 1985; Borgen and Shade 1984). Collaborative research on business climates and manpower needs is crucial to enhancing stature because developing questionnaires and procedures for interviews requires substantial cooperation among agencies. Cooperative undertaking of these procedures results in shared understanding of products, operations, and needs among for-profit and nonprofit organizations.

Colleges and universities are also surveying the parents of undergraduate students to learn what types of information they want and expect from the college. Survey research conducted with 1,499 parents of Princeton University students in 1985 indicated that parents wanted personalized communications from the university, they wanted to attend classes, they wanted to learn about the curriculum and academic advising, and they wanted to attend programs in their home communities featuring faculty speakers or student groups from campus rather than a local alumni gathering (Halsey 1985).

Some institutions use alumni surveys to improve stature by eliciting information that can be used to improve the fit between alumni interests and institutional programs and services (Pendel 1985). Knowing personal characteristics of alumni—careers and educational history; activities with professional, government, military, and religious organizations; board memberships; honors, achievements, publications, or creative works; spouse's career and educational history, board memberships, activities, achievements, and awards; income; reflections on experiences at the undergraduate institution, evaluation of the education received, and current impressions of the institution; and willingness to use influence on behalf of the institution—colleges have improved support by engaging alumni as partners in institutional development (Pendel 1985). For example, alumni at the peak of their professional lives have become an important source of information for academic advisors, deans, department chairs, and faculty about the impact of changes in the world of work on the undergraduate curriculum.

Finally, colleges and state systems of higher education have published information in the form of master plans and goal statements that improve stature by demonstrating responsiveness to constituents' needs. Responding to a challenge in 1983 by the governor to give him "a plan for higher education that will really make a difference in Oregon," the Oregon State System of Higher Education developed a precise statement of goals for system institutions based on assessment of strengths and weaknesses, identification of potential new areas of excellence, and determination of state and regional postsecondary education needs (Davis 1986). A strategic plan was issued and position papers were developed for use with legislators, legislative candidates, organized lobbies, publishers, and media representatives to build support for the plan. Similar practices to enhance stature based on a principle of "information and involvement" have been employed in New York by the State Education Department and in Illinois by the Board of Higher Education.

Constituents' involvement in campus activities

The literature on college advancement stresses the importance of constituents' involvement in campus activities (see, for example, Topor 1985). In the lexicon of administrators, groups that contribute resources to the institution—students, parents, state legislators, and alumni—will elevate their impression of the institution if they spend time on campus, participate in activities, and have direct contact with faculty and administrators. Traditional revenue providers like parents, alumni, and government agency officials are more reluctant than yesterday's consumers to provide unquestioned support to higher education. They talk in terms of accountability and have strong needs for information about the benefits of higher education, such as personal enrichment, career development, socioeconomic mobility, and improvement in the quality of life (Yankelovich 1987). The question is, then, how can colleges meaningfully involve important constituencies in institutional activities? And, in turn, how can these constituencies educate colleges to be more in tune with the rudiments of stature in their world? To many administrators, involvement of external constituencies in campus activities means special programming for prospective students (like campus visits) to fill the entering class for next year. Indeed, most, if not all, colleges have campus visitation programs for prospective students (Rubins 1985). Some colleges have expanded programming to include parents both before and during their child's attendance at college. San Diego State University (SDSU) operates its Parents Orientation Program to acclimate parents to specific features of academic life (Holmes, Miller, and Varon 1985). A typical orientation program includes a discussion on academics led by the vice president for academic affairs, a discussion on student development led by student services staff, smaller sessions for in-depth discussion on topics such as placement and financial aid, and informal discussions with upperclassmen. When parents were asked to rate from poor to excellent their feelings about SDSU before attending the orientation program and after, the result was a dramatic increase to the positive; 66 percent moved in a positive direction, and only 1 percent moved to the negative.

A growing number of institutions have sought to involve alumni in campus activities to improve visibility and support. A 1975 survey showed that 57 percent of a sample of 327 colleges and universities sponsored some type of educational activity for their graduates (Gilbert 1985). Interest in alumni programming has increased in recent years, as colleges have looked at specific demographic trends:

- In 1985, adults who were 25 to 45 years of age made up 31 percent of the population in the United States.
- One-third of all American adults take part in some type of adult continuing education.
- The more educated an adult is, the more likely he or she will want to undertake continuous learning to facilitate personal growth.
- Adults at the peak of their professional careers have strong needs for affiliation and a sense of community; they participate in a network of personal and professional relationships that can be enormously beneficial to colleges (Yankelovich 1987).

Alumni involvement in educational programs takes many forms, both on and off campus: lectures at club meetings, panel discussions and academic lectures during reunion weekends, travel programs that feature continuing education, career development programs, "alumni days" that specifically address topics of interest to special groups, and learning vacations on campus or at some university-owned retreat. Learning vacations or alumni colleges are the most visible and prevalent forms of alumni involvement in campus activities (Gilbert 1985). Perhaps the most extensive program of this kind is Cornell's Adult University, which runs five weeks each summer and attracts both alumni and nonalumni to a variety of educational programs.

Finally, some institutions have attempted to improve stature with public officials and those who make funding decisions by inviting legislators to campus. In addition to visits made to campus for special events (ground-breaking ceremonies, graduation exercises, fund-raising events, for example), several colleges have established a legislator visitation program. Legislators spend a day on campus, attend classes, talk with students and faculty about curriculum and instruction, and receive a briefing from administrators about strategic facets of management, such as finance and planning. The University of California has established the Legislator to Campus Program through which state and federal lawmakers come to campus to learn about research of interest to them and their constituents (Hooper 1984). The program gives legislators a direct, nonfiscal perspective on what the university does with state appropriations. Active research on health, education, and state and national economic issues has been shown to be of interest to legislators because of the impact the research may have on their constituents (Hooper 1984). The objective is to ensure that elected officials better understand how appropriations are spent and the ways in which college teaching, research, and service benefit the public.

Outreach activities bringing the campus to constituencies

In the last decade or so, curricula have swung toward more electives, more alternatives, and less structure (Baldridge, Kemerer, and Green 1982). Along with the flexibility in curricula has come expansion of outreach activities to nontraditional students. Colleges have taken courses and services into the community, they have placed greater emphasis on the use of media in marketing, and they have spent more time cultivating important constituencies in off-campus locations. Administrators have discovered that outreach is an important ingredient in determining stature.

Community-based educational programs focused on localities as centers of organized ethnic, racial, religious, social, and cultural groups represent the fullest expression of outreach in colleges and universities. Frequently, these programs involve negotiations for modifying the general educational program and for tailoring new forms of higher education to the particular needs of special-interest groups. Community-based programming provides a powerful base for the enhancement of stature. It builds allegiance among community interest groups by providing opportunities for nontraditional learners, it generates publicity and visibility for the college, and it provides resources other than tax levies for college operations (Hyland 1984). The flow between college and community aids in providing an outward thrust for institutional development and helps citizens become aware of the benefits of postsecondary education.

A growing number of institutions are using the media to deliver messages about the value of their programs and services. Radio news services, radio services, radio paid advertising, radio public service announcements, educational television, and television advertising are used to disseminate information to the public (Raley 1984). The Clemson University Radio News Service, for example, uses a telephone answering device connected to a dedicated telephone line to provide national radio stations with "Clemson Feeds." Clemson provides callers with a "wrap" (a quick story ready for airing) and two "cuts" (activities that relate to the wrap), allowing callers to package news to their needs (Crockett 1984). Northeastern University Radio Network offers free broadcast-quality news features to callers in a nine-state region to increase public awareness and improve public opinion of the institution (McLeod 1984). The University of Minnesota's *Newsline* offers hard news, perspectives on the news, consumer information, agricultural news, weather reports, feature reports on research, and coverage of visiting lecturers, dignitaries, and women's athletics as a public service to callers (Elton 1984). Penn State University, focusing on low-cost/high-impact radio, uses "Interview Possibility" sheets to guide radio stations to breaking events, research findings, and services on campus. Each week, Penn State's radio/TV section sends a sheet to Pennsylvania stations and others across the nation focused on one topic, a brief description, and the source for additional information—generally a faculty member or administrator (Stober 1984)—a technique that has led to national radio coverage for the university.

Some institutions have used media to improve stature with a particular sector, such as potential students and parents. Washington University in St. Louis mails audio tapes each month to some 80 radio stations that broadcast in areas where large numbers of prospective students live (Kraushaar 1984). This news feature service offers two- to three-minute feature stories based on current scholarly activity and research projects at the university. The University of Florida produces a daily 110-second program about general-interest, health-related topics, featuring interviews with faculty members from the College of Medicine (Buck 1984). In a continuing radio series entitled "You and Your Child," the University of Kansas attempts to reach young adults by providing tips on child raising on such topics as managing shopping trips with youngsters, children's toys, and keeping preschoolers from going out on the street (Barthell 1984). Montana State University uses television to present information about institutional research to high school students on the benefits of attending college (Hample 1985). The goals of these and other media techniques are to increase familiarity and name recognition of the institution, to present information about college purposes in an entertaining, easy-to-understand way, and to showcase the benefits of teaching, research, and public service so as to enhance the stature of the institution.

Anticipating volatility in enrollments and funding sources into the 1990s, most colleges have attempted to diversify revenue by expanding outreach to major donors. They have also intensified their lobbying efforts with traditional revenue providers, such as state legislatures and federal agencies. Many colleges are using automated programs with sophisticated reporting capability to cultivate major donors, planning and documenting interaction with donors (Turner et al. 1984). Using routinely available structured data base management systems combined with such formating programs as Reportwriter, institutions have generated data about donors that can be used to guide and support outreach. A personal dimension has been added through the direct involvement of deans, faculty, and students in cultivating donors and alumni. At American University, faculty members and deans are invited to major events that include donors and alumni (D'Agostino 1985). They are asked to share lists of alumni and influential persons with whom they correspond, they are sent copies of press releases announcing promotions of former students, and they are responsible for identifying and facilitating contact with prospective donors and alumni volunteers. South Florida University uses "student ambassadors" to strengthen relations with donors and community groups (Patouillet 1986). Appointed annually by the college president, 20 ambassadors participate in major activities of the Greater Tampa Chamber of Commerce, speak to local civic clubs, work with top business leaders, help out with gubernatorial debates, and serve as hosts for college activities in the community—all for the purpose of improving the image of the institution with important constituencies.

Colleges and universities seeking to gain leverage in decisions affecting appropriations are reaching out to state legislators and federal officials through lobbying. Most institutions employ several basic strategies: (1) identifying and contacting key policy makers, (2) holding special events to heighten awareness of the institution's performance and needs, (3) selecting and cultivating sponsors for legislation, (4) developing and distributing descriptive material to key individuals, and (5) monitoring votes to ensure attention to college needs and interests (Troxler and Jarrell 1984). Some institutions have engaged alumni in lobbying to achieve important goals related to stature. The University of California, for example, has established the Alumni Association Legislative Network to provide assistance in lobbying in selective dealings with the California legislature (Hooper 1984). Alumni in professions that are regulated or have a close tie to government (lawyers, physicians, realtors, and insurance agents) are pressed into service on specific bills or on events through which the university wants to communicate its importance to the economic and social growth of the state.

Published assessment data describing college performance
Growing federal and state interest in assessment has forced colleges and universities to direct more money, time, and expertise to research on student outcomes. Faced with the prospect that information about student outcomes will become more important in state agencies' deliberations about resources, students' enrollment decisions, and the efforts of faculty to improve teaching and learning, administrators have initiated campus-based assessment programs. Three examples of comprehensive institutional assessment programs are reported in the following paragraphs.[1]

Northeast Missouri State University. Northeast Missouri State University's assessment program, frequently called the value-added assessment program, seeks to serve three purposes: (1) to demonstrate that NMSU makes a positive impact on students' lives; (2) to demonstrate that students who graduate from NMSU are competitive in terms of knowledge, skills, and personal development; and (3) to ensure that NMSU administrators and faculty will know everything possible about their students.

To fulfill these three purposes, the institution developed a comprehensive data base that includes information about several factors:

- Students' academic and personal backgrounds before entering college;

1. The descriptions of institutional assessment programs at Northeast Missouri State University, Alverno College, and the University of Tennessee at Knoxville are based on Nettles 1987.

- Students' academic and extracurricular activities while in college and all students' postcollegiate educational and professional activities as alumni;
- Students' performance on college entrance examinations when entering college and after completing the sophomore year; and
- Students' performance on licensure examinations, such as the NTE and the American Institute of Certified Public Accountants achievement exam or the GRE subject tests just before graduating with a baccalaureate degree.

The assessment program has focused the attention of publics outside the university on the university's demonstrated performance, not simply the resources it requires to operate or the costs of education.

Alverno College. Alverno College is a small, private liberal arts college for women, located in Milwaukee, Wisconsin, with an enrollment of 1,500 undergraduate students. In 1973, the faculty developed an assessment program that would be informative to each individual student about progress toward achieving the college's curriculum objectives. These curriculum objectives are eight intellectual skills that students will use throughout life: communication, analysis, problem solving, valuing, social interaction, taking environmental responsibility, involvement in the contemporary world, and aesthetic response.

The methods for assessing students' achievement of these skills are multifaceted, and they include written and oral presentations and experiments. A typical assessment at Alverno is for a student to view a film and write a paragraph and/or give an oral interpretation of its contents. The assessments are mostly designed by faculty at Alverno and judged by Alverno faculty and professionals in the business community of Milwaukee who have no official affiliation with the college. Alverno avoids using externally developed instruments except occasionally to compare its students' performance with those of other institutions. The eight skills are interwoven into every course, and assessment is part of every course in addition to regular course examination. Students receive continuous formal feedback during personal interviews with faculty.

University of Tennessee at Knoxville. The University of Tennessee at Knoxville (UTK) is a major land-grant research university with 20,000 undergraduate students and 6,000 graduate and professional students. The university has a comprehensive student assessment program encompassing annual administration of a test of general education to a sample of entering freshmen and a sample of graduating seniors to measure growth in general education over the course of the curriculum; assessment of achievement in major fields using licensure exams, subject exams of the GRE, and tests developed by faculty for fields in which no outside examinations are available; and administration of an instrument called the Student Satisfaction Survey, which was developed by faculty and staff at UTK to assess students' opinions about the quality of academic programs and services of the university.

Faculty at the university have used the results of these assessments to improve student advising, to improve courses, to solve course scheduling problems, and to improve course content where students needed help based upon the results of their tests. Because the state of Tennessee rewards the institution for conducting the assessment and for achieving positive outcomes, UTK received $1.2 million in 1982, the first year of the program. The amount of the award increased to $2.9 million in 1983 because of improved performance and to $3.5 million in 1984.

These programs are the exception rather than the rule: Most institutions have not implemented comprehensive assessment programs. And in the institutions where assessment data are available, administrators are reluctant to convert these data into published marketing materials like catalogs, student handbooks, program bulletins, and student recruiting materials. Effective use of assessment data has been in situations where institutions stand to achieve important gains through the selective use of information. Consider, for example, the strategy employed by Ball State University to acquire legislative support for University College in 1985–86.[2]

Before 1985, Ball State University was facing a student attrition rate of 60 percent between matriculation and graduation. A study of attrition factors found that two groups of students were most at risk: those academically underprepared for college work and those undecided about a major. To improve retention

The assessment program has focused the attention of publics outside the university on the university's demonstrated performance, not simply the resources it requires to operate or the costs of education.

2. The description of the political strategy employed at Ball State University for development and support of University College is excerpted from Weaver, Stevenson, and Thompson 1986.

among these groups without compromising academic standards, University College (UC) was established to provide a comprehensive program of advising, assessment, and academic support for the target group: approximately 1,500 undecided and underprepared freshmen. Although legislative funding for this initiative was denied for the 1985–87 biennium, the program was funded through the internal reallocation of resources. Therefore, the UC program was undertaken in a politically charged climate, lacking state support and having "usurped" monies from other colleges and departments on campus.

Ball State University is a public, residential university with an enrollment of 18,000 students and an emphasis on undergraduate education. The majority of students are Indiana residents, and the majority of them are first-generation college students. Although Indiana is slightly above the national average in the percentage of its population who are high school graduates (65.9 percent), in 1980 it ranked 47th in percent of adults with four years of college or more (12.4 percent). The quality of secondary and postsecondary education has been under attack, particularly as the declining industrial basis of the state's economy has resulted in a strong economic argument for increasing the number of residents who seek and who complete postsecondary degrees. University College arose in the midst of the debate over access and excellence, however, and the Indiana Commission on Higher Education (ICHE) determined to promote excellence by limiting access. In its 1985 annual report, ICHE recommended that (1) statewide "basic skills" standards and tests be established to govern admission to state universities; (2) college-level basic skills programs be identified as a separate category within university operating budgets; and (3) by 1990 no students be admitted unconditionally to state universities who have not demonstrated competence in basic skills. The ICHE intended to define "remedial" education and to eliminate it from postsecondary institutions. According to ICHE's public statements, college-level remediation was targeted for elimination, and University College was widely, though falsely, perceived to be remedial in nature. A clear purpose and demonstrated effectiveness were thus essential to UC's survival.

University College research protocol calls for comparison of retention data and academic performance (as measured by grade point averages) among freshmen matriculants entering Ball State University during three academic years (1984–85,

1985–86, 1986–87). A pre–University College cohort was established to include underprepared (admitted "on warning") and undecided students who matriculated in 1984–85 before University College services were available. Retention and performance data for this cohort were compared to 1985–86, and undecided, on warning, and both undecided and on warning students were identified and their performances compared. Supplementing these data were studies of specific University College activities (for example, academic advising, peer tutoring, career counseling) and studies of UC students using such measures as the ACT/COMP test, the Myers-Briggs Type Indicator, and the Survey of Study Habits and Attitudes.

University College programs have resulted in dramatically improved rates of retention among UC students, compared with the pre-UC cohort. While every UC subgroup has shown improved retention, the undecided students show the greatest effects: a 22 percent gain in number completing the first year; a 19 percent gain in number returning for the second year; and a 28 percent gain in number completing the second year. Although UC students achieved grade point averages slightly below those for their non-UC counterparts in the same freshman class, they have outperformed the pre-UC cohort and met university criteria for retention. Statewide policies were affected by this demonstrated impact. The Indiana General Assembly did fund University College programs for the 1987–89 biennium. Further, legislators supported new initiatives for a freshman year experience program and a model of excellence in undergraduate education, both developed within UC. Additionally, the ICHE has begun to recognize a distinction for "precollege remediation" programs for students who are admissible but need help in making the transition from high school or the workplace to college.

Influence of leaders' behavior on public opinion
An oft-repeated idiom in higher education is that "institutions take on the characteristics of their leaders." After all, leaders relate the institution to the public, perform a pivotal role in budget decisions, establish strategic plans for the institution, maintain authority for program development and elimination, and provide the organizational climate necessary to produce societally valued outcomes in students. A 1974 study of college and university presidents found that most leaders characterized their roles as a mixture of administrator (dealing with hierarchi-

cal subordinates), political leader (dealing with constituents), and entrepreneur (dealing with workers, customers, and suppliers) (Cohen and March 1974). The modern leader must rely heavily on functional authority—that is, authority based on competence, experience, relations incorporating mutual influence and trust, skill in leadership, greater possession of information, and personal persuasiveness (Mortimer and McConnell 1982). In other words, the leader must legitimate his or her authority by securing and keeping affirmative support from the institution's constituencies.

The notion of legitimacy through support of constituencies lies at the heart of institutional efforts to improve stature through the leader's persona. Governing boards have discovered that institutional performance and ultimately public opinion depend greatly on the leader's behavior. Increasingly, the leader's capacity to see the organization as a system of functions, membership groups, and decision-making processes interacting with manifold external forces will become a determinant of institutional stature (Mortimer and McConnell 1982). Perhaps the need to understand how stature is produced through the relationship between leader, organizational behavior, and external forces is one reason that, even as early as the late 1970s, the focus on leadership style shifted to the transactional leader. The transactional leader mobilizes various social, economic, technological, and political resources to realize goals that may be independent or mutually held by followers (Burns 1978). A college or university president continually exchanges potential for influence in the shaping of institutional goals for affirmative support of constituencies. Values of transactional leadership relate to the manner of this exchange with emphasis on honesty, responsibility, honoring of commitments, and fairness.

How does leadership demonstrated by a president and/or governing board in a specific organizational context determine institutional stature? Consider the example of Southern Methodist University in its recent presidential search following a devastating athletic scandal in 1986.[3]

3. Material describing the presidential search at Southern Methodist University is excerpted from the *Chronicle of Higher Education*, 10 June 1987, pp. 35–36 and from an unpublished paper by Judith Pitney, "Improving Institutional Image through the President's Persona: A Case Study of Southern Methodist University in 1987."

Southern Methodist University, before 1986, was a comprehensive southwestern university on the rise according to market factors traditionally associated with a favorable image in higher education. Enrollments were increasing, two schools, theology and law, were ranked nationally in the top 20, new endowed chairs were added and filled between 1982 and 1986, the combined SAT score of entering freshmen was improving, and the university's endowment more than tripled between 1981 and 1986.

Then news of the football scandal reached the media. Charges of illegal payments to football players were proven to the satisfaction of the National Collegiate Athletic Association in November 1986. The football coach, athletic director, and president resigned. It was soon discovered that Texas Governor William P. Clements and SMU's Board of Governors were involved in the scandal. What many inside and outside the university had long feared was soon proven: That decision making was dominated by a small group of Dallas businessmen whose priorities did not necessarily coincide with those of the faculty or administration.

The university was in turmoil. Public confidence in the university had eroded, reflected by the decline in the number of applications for admission and a decrease in private gifts and donations. In the midst of this turmoil, a newly appointed presidential search committee set to work. The search process was designed to begin to rebuild public confidence by identifying a leader with an impeccable track record in academic management and with scholarly credentials.

From a field of 228 candidates, A. Kenneth Pye, a professor of law and former acting president and chancellor of Duke University, was selected as the new president. Pye had earned a reputation as a brilliant administrator unafraid to make unpopular decisions. He had helped Duke recover from a period of retrenchment to become one of the finest universities in the South. The SMU community was confident he would be able to do the same at SMU and to build stature in the process.

College presidents differ in their background experience and style of leadership. Like corporate executives, they are the identifying mark for the institution. Their actions are closely watched by the public and their behavior—verbal and nonverbal—viewed as a reflection of the institution. Those presidents who understand the interplay among executive, institution, and external environment find that public perceptions of the institution may rise or fall in relationship to their performance. While they are particularly sensitive to the dual and sometimes conflicting requirements for leadership by groups within and without the college, presidents and other executives voice a need for better understanding of the relationship between the leader's behavior and public perception.

Summary

Colleges and universities have concentrated on five methods to enhance institutional stature with their constituencies: (1) institutional information demonstrating sensitivity to clients' needs, (2) involvement of constituencies in campus activities, (3) outreach activities bringing the campus to constituencies, (4) published assessment data describing college performance, and (5) behavior of the leader to influence public opinion. A few institutions have grasped the importance of institutional stature and have designed and implemented strategies to enhance it. The majority, however, concentrate on short-term marketing practices that rely solely on communication. These institutions overlook the importance of the dimensions that contribute to stature. The next section briefly outlines techniques that address each dimension of stature and that colleges and universities can implement to enhance stature.

What Colleges Are Not Doing

Stature is a multidimensional phenomenon, and institutions do not control many of the factors that contribute to stature. To illustrate, colleges and universities can influence the number and quality of students enrolled, the policies and standards regulating academic programs and students' performance, and the quality of staff hired to teach students. They cannot, however, influence the tempo of social change and the general direction of public opinion. Likewise, colleges and universities operate differently from other types of organizations. As loosely coupled, labor-intensive organizations with ambiguous goals, they may resist an orientation toward consumers. They seek stature because it is an affirmation of the quality of faculty and staff, not of the performance of the institution in satisfying consumers' needs. In short, colleges may be limited in the techniques that they can use to enhance stature by the very characteristics of the academic organization.

Using the conceptual model, analysis of public opinion, and practices of complex organizations discussed earlier as a framework for analysis, what practices have colleges and universities neglected that are important in enhancing stature? Improvements in stature can be carried out in four areas: strategic assessment, allocation of resources, outcomes assessment, and image management.

Strategic assessment

College and university administrators do not fully understand the relationship between their institutions and features of the broader environment. Although interest in "environmental scanning" has increased in recent years, a select few institutions have implemented comprehensive systems for surveying the environment, selecting key environmental trends and issues for concentrated tracking, and channeling important issues into the strategic decision process (Hearn and Heydinger 1985). Moreover, higher education institutions have neither the resources nor the expertise to conduct ongoing research on public opinion.

Efforts to scan and monitor the external environment are not supported by data management systems inside the college. Many institutions have undergone a process of serial change in their management information systems to remain abreast of the latest technology. Serial change places the emphasis in information systems on the mechanics of operating the system rather than on the information required to support strategic decisions. The result is a management information system deficient in the systematic collection of information needed to make decisions that carefully relate the institution to its environment. Information from outside the institution flows into the system on a random and piecemeal basis, while information from inside the institution is collected on the basis of convenience—a circumstance that hampers the capacity of managers to acquire early warnings of change in external conditions or internal capability.

How is it possible that colleges and universities cannot comprehend their external environment because of poorly developed systems for strategic assessment? Consider the example of institutions that combine any number of the following characteristics:

- A system for strategic decision making centered in the president's cabinet that serves to restrict use of information generated by lower levels in the organization;
- A fragmented approach to institutional research, with mul-

tiple offices and individuals performing the function and each defining it a different way;

- Serial change in the hardware and software technology used to drive the management information systems, serving to produce incompatibility between historical and current data bases;
- A disciplinary organization that shreds the relationship of the whole institution to the environment;
- Vague and diffuse institutional goals, which pose difficulty to institutions in sorting environmental stimuli into "relevant" and "irrelevant";
- Bias toward convenience and caution in information gathering, which focuses environmental assessment on a limited pool of information;
- Resistance to change among faculty and staff impelled to protect the academic "integrity" of the institution in periods of social change;
- Lack of financial resources and qualified staff to establish and sustain environmental scanning and monitoring programs.

Systems for strategic assessment comprised of environmental scanning and monitoring programs, a coordinated program of institutional research, management information systems that integrate historical and current data bases using modern technology, and management networks that integrate information from different parts of the institution in the strategic decision process are a missing and important dimension of colleges' and universities' efforts to enhance stature.

Allocation of resources

It is reasonable to expect that if environmental scanning and monitoring is to become a significant force in enhancing stature, efforts must be also made to incorporate the results of scanning (information) into the budgetary process. Most colleges have not established comprehensive planning systems and mechanisms for feedback to channel information from the environment into decisions affecting the allocation of resources. Decision making has not been timely in relationship to major changes in the environment, leading publics to ask whether a lag exists between institutional programs and consumers' needs (Hearn and Heydinger 1985). Realigning institutions with their

environments is a difficult task, because resources are not always sufficient to permit comprehensive development.

Outcomes assessment

A strong program for outcomes assessment is a requisite for enhancing stature in colleges and universities. In the absence of
information about the outcomes and benefits of postsecondary
education, the public has no basis on which to judge costs and
value. An examination of long-term outcomes and careful integration of academic programs with students' needs will increase
stature as students' satisfaction increases. This overall goal has
not been realized on many campuses, however. Colleges have
undertaken only piecemeal and sporadic efforts to measure outcomes (Ewell 1987).

First, most institutions have focused efforts at assessment on
the academic characteristics and skills of entering students.
They know the high school GPA, achievement test scores, and
proficiency in basic skills of entering students. The majority of
institutions have information on students' persistence and performance in college, which means they are aware of attrition
and retention rates, course completion and performance, and
graduation rates. Most colleges do not as a rule, however, conduct annual studies of student outcomes in work, further education, and community following termination of study (Alfred
1987). Administrators cannot easily respond to questions concerning the near-term and long-term employment patterns of
graduates (job titles, salaries, job promotions, honors and
awards, relationship of job to curriculum, students' satisfaction
with curriculum and instruction, employers' satisfaction with
graduates, and so on), further education (credits completed in
other institutions, advanced degrees, performance on graduate
and professional examinations, academic honors, for example),
and the quality of life (involvement in community organizations, improved family life, participation in elections, for example). Many institutions have recognized this fact and are
making efforts to overcome it through research programs designed to collect follow-up data from students. These efforts
come late and often in response to prodding from government
agencies and revenue providers. Their immediate utility as a
strategy to enhance stature will be limited.

Second, colleges do not have a fundamental understanding of
value addedness. The public policy agendas of government
agencies and officials suggest that evidence of value addedness

will become an increasingly important factor in the choice of a college and resource decisions. Defined as the differential between a student's potential for success at the time of entry to college (as reflected in the entering student's characteristics) and actual student outcomes attained as a result of college attendance, value addedness is a difficult argument for colleges to mount with external constituencies (Ohio Board of Regents 1987). Ambiguous goals make formation of the concept difficult, and variation in academic objectives across departments and disciplines makes institutionwide measurement a cumbersome task.

College officials claim that they cannot measure the outcomes of college attendance with any degree of confidence because they cannot isolate the effects of education from the effects contributed by other groups, organizations, and social institutions. Measurement can most easily be attempted in relationship to near-term indicators directly related to college attendance, such as first job after college or enrollment in advanced-degree institutions. Consequently, most colleges limit outcomes assessment to analysis of the near-term direct effects of education.

Image management
The management of image in colleges and universities is almost always resource driven (Topor 1986). Whether publications and other forms of communication are designed to recruit students, to increase appropriations and gifts, or to improve an institution's visibility with important publics, a decline in institutional "resources" (students, money, or visibility) is perceived as symptomatic of a problem with image. Institutions scramble to develop new marketing techniques, some as simple as redesigning institutional publications, others as complex as reorganizing administration to improve public affairs management. The bottom line is that image management—some would call it public relations—has become a burgeoning area of concern in college and university administration.

Conclusion
An important assumption of the model presented in the first section is that institutional stature is a product of institutional attributes, performance, and outputs that match the needs and expectations of important constituencies. Needs and expectations may change as societal conditions change, but they are

always present and they must be systematically addressed. The description of college and university practices in this section reveals that most institutions focus strategies to enhance stature on formal and informal communication with specific constituencies about college programs and services. Several important trends emerge from this description:

- Only recently have colleges and universities begun to collect systematic information about public needs, expectations, and perceptions of postsecondary education. The information that is available often is not critically examined or effectively integrated into decision making.
- Institutional communications describing resources (programs, services, facilities, research, and staff) available to external constituencies are clearly the most often used public affairs strategy. Institutions do not systematically collect information about student outcomes; if this information is collected, it is selectively used in communications, leading to a distorted image of college operations.
- Public affairs officials do not systematically incorporate forms of language, thought patterns, and frames of reference used by the public in college publications. Important information provided through institutional goal statements, program descriptions, and financial reports is written for the benefit of educators, not the general public.

It is apparent that most institutions have not done much to communicate openly and comprehensively with the public. A major reason is that until recently colleges and universities were viewed as having characteristics that made them different from other types of organizations. As such, they were not called upon to communicate in precise detail about their goals, products, performance, costs, and spending behavior. This lack of attention to detail is a tragic oversight.

Colleges and universities are not doing all they can to enhance stature through organizational practices—a particularly ironic situation, because institutions can control public opinion to a certain extent through information only they can provide. This section has briefly reviewed the practices that institutions use to promote themselves to the public and problem areas that will require attention if stature is to improve. Strategies to enhance stature will not be effective, however, until colleges and universities address some underlying problems in management. This topic is the focus of the remaining section.

ORGANIZING COLLEGES AND UNIVERSITIES TO ENHANCE STATURE

The primary concern of this monograph is to determine what strategies and actions colleges and universities must take to enhance stature. Identifying workable strategies to enhance stature is not an easy task. Multiple relationships exist among the dimensions of stature, leading to difficulty in measuring the effects of specific strategies. Furthermore, college and university administrators do not have a comprehensive understanding of how stature develops and its multiple antecedents. Thus, how can administrators develop effective strategies for a phenomenon they do not fully understand?

College and university administrators do not have a comprehensive understanding of how stature develops and its multiple antecedents.

The objective of the model in figure 1 was to identify major dimensions of college and university stature and to examine the most important of these dimensions in individual sections. Three dimensions were identified, each describing important features of the relationship between higher education institutions and the larger environment: societal conditions, the needs, expectations, and opinions of external constituencies, and organizational attributes and performance. A review of practices to enhance stature employed by complex organizations revealed four categories of practices with potential application to higher education: (1) relating organizational products and services to consumers' needs, (2) allocating resources for development and improvement of organizational products, (3) assessing the quality and benefits of organizational products, and (4) advancing organizational image with important constituencies. When examined in context with the organizational and performance attributes of colleges and universities, these practices suggest several spheres of activity that can become the focus of efforts to enhance stature:

- Management of the effects of societal change on institutional programs, services, and resources through environmental scanning, monitoring, and strategic planning *(Strategic Assessment)*;
- Improvement of institutional responsiveness to changing external conditions through resource allocation systems that incorporate mechanisms for planning, feedback, and innovation *(Allocation of Resources)*;
- Collection and publication of information about benefits and costs that describes institutional and student outcomes, expenditures, and costs as a means for demonstrating accountability to important constituencies *(Outcomes Assessment)*;

- Management of public opinion through assessment of the effectiveness of institutional marketing and public relations techniques, coupled with redesign of organizational communication strategies to create impact with constituencies *(Image Management)*.

A message often repeated in this report is that colleges and universities have little control over many factors that contribute to institutional stature. They have little influence over societal conditions, the general direction of public policy, and public confidence in social institutions. By contrast, colleges can borrow from successful practices in complex organizations to create changes in operations and performance that engender positive perceptions with the public.

A reexamination of the practices of complex organizations presented earlier (see table 5, pp. 55–58) points to a number of practices that colleges can employ to improve stature within the spheres of activity presented above. These practices are listed and described in table 6, and they provide a framework for the discussion of leveraging strategies that follows.

The assumption underlying these activity domains is that as institutions come to better understand how societal forces, public opinion, and organizational behavior interact to determine stature, they will move to develop strategies that result in enhanced stature. Most institutions, prodded by recent criticism, have begun to develop marketing and public relations plans. Much energy is expended on these plans—with mixed results. After examining what the literature has to say about practices in complex organizations and public affairs strategies employed by colleges and universities, we have become convinced that many of these strategies are cosmetic. They attack the symptoms of the problem, but they do not address the problem itself. Instead of piecemeal public relations efforts with selected constituencies, it would be wiser to develop a coordinated strategy for enhancement involving these activity domains. Instead of vesting too much faith in marketing and public relations plans that often do little more than temporarily appease certain constituencies, institutions can improve stature by altering their approach to management. The goal is this: Develop assessment and communication systems that enable institutions to effectively anticipate and respond to external forces while simultaneously educating the public about important goals, purposes, outcomes, and benefits of postsecondary education. It is not

TABLE 6
ACTIVITY DOMAINS AND PRACTICES TO ENHANCE STATURE IN COLLEGES AND UNIVERSITIES

Activity Domains and Practices	Description	Practices of Complex Organizations
Strategic Assessment	*Management of the effects of societal change on institutional programs, services, and resources through environmental scanning, monitoring, and strategic planning*	*Relating organizational products and services to consumers' needs*
• Environmental scanning, monitoring, and strategic planning	Assessment and monitoring of issues and trends of organizationwide significance (sociocultural, demographic, economic, public policy, political, and technological) that present challenges, opportunities, and threats to the institution; synthesis of environmental information into a strategic plan that aligns the institution with specific features of its external environment	Product visibility; orientation toward serving client; timely strategic decisions
• Institutional research/market research	Continuous information-gathering program with target audiences to determine specific needs and expectations for postsecondary education	
• Management information systems	Organized information systems internal to the institution that can be used to guide and support strategic decisions by providing current and historical data about institutional costs, resources, outcomes, and performance	

TABLE 6 (continued)

Allocation of Resources	*Improvement of institutional responsiveness to external conditions through modified resource allocation systems*	*Allocating resources for development and improvement of products and services*
• Integrated evaluation and budgeting systems	Administrative organization for planning and budgeting that supports continuous and timely infusion of results of evaluation into financial decisions	Distinctiveness in products, services, and operations; capacity for innovation
• Support for innovation	Institutional policies guiding use of discretionary resources to support innovation (programs and services)	
Outcomes Assessment	*Collection and publication of information about costs and benefits as a means of demonstrating institutional accountability to important constituencies*	*Assessing the quality, appeal, and benefits of organizational products and services*
• Comprehensive outcomes assessment	Annual or biannual program for assessment of near-term and long-term student outcomes in work, further education, leisure, family community, political life, etc.	Continuous performance assessment; management of cost sensitivity
• Beneficiaries' satisfaction	Assessment of beneficiaries' perceptions (students, business and industry officials, community residents, state agency officials, parents, etc.) of the quality and value of educational programs and services before, during, and after contact with the college	

TABLE 6 (continued)

• Cost management	Assessment of the "psychic costs" associated with college attendance—the point at which costs outweigh benefits in the minds of specific individuals, groups, and organizations	
• Documentation of spending behavior	Periodic publication of information for consumers describing how the institution spends money over a given period of time	
• Progress marketing	Development of marketing information with a focus on students' near-term and long-term outcomes of college attendance in contrast to a focus on institutional resources available to consumer groups	
Image Management	*Management of public opinion through assessment of institutional marketing and public relations techniques and redesign of communication strategies*	*Advancing organizational image with important constituencies*
• Image profile	Systematic review of all outreach materials created and used by an institution to represent itself in particular ways to target audiences	Financial durability and soundness; community and environmental responsibility; response to pressure situations; demonstrated expertise in communications
• Capacity for distinctiveness	Representation in marketing materials of special features implicit in institutional programs, services, operations, and outcomes that distinguish the institution from competitors	

TABLE 6 (continued)

• Simplified unique goals	Simplification of institutional goal statements, presentation in lay language, and repetition to improve public's understanding and support
• Opinion management	Audit of public opinion in relationship to institutional programs, operations, and performance, leading to the determination of "desirable" opinions, attitudes, and perceptions to be reinforced through institutional publications
• Media monitoring	Continuous monitoring of various media to identify opinions, attitudes, and perceptions held in relationship to higher education in general and local institutions in particular
• Crisis communication management	Written plan guiding the flow and coordination of communication from the institution to the public in periods of organizational stress
• Research on effective communication	Assessment of the impact of institutional publications and outreach strategies on specific constituencies

sufficient for the purposes of enhancing stature simply to alter institutional programs and services based on information about the future. Stature will accrue to those institutions that convincingly demonstrate how they provide benefits to individuals, groups, and organizations that satisfy important needs and goals.

Leveraging Strategies: Strategic Assessment
History indicates that institutions of higher education have been slow to adapt to changes in their environment, especially their

resource markets. The model and the practices of complex organizations discussed earlier point to a need for assessment to determine the extent of congruence between environmental forces and institutional activities. After all, if colleges and universities are to lay claim to stature, their goals, plans, operations, and outcomes must somehow correspond to environmental forces, and they must satisfy the expectations of constituents.

Environmental scanning, monitoring, and strategic planning
The time has come to employ the techniques of environmental scanning, monitoring, and strategic planning used in the business sector, and colleges and universities are in fact beginning to develop systems for scanning the environment and strategic planning (Keller 1983). Environmental scanning has often been a quick-and-dirty attempt to prepare an agency-mandated overview of trends in the institutional service region to qualify for funding. As colleges and universities move into a period of intensified public scrutiny of goals, performance, and costs, the sophistication of environmental scanning, strategic planning, management information systems, and institutional research will need to improve.

What form should environmental scanning take and how should it be combined with strategic planning, management information systems, and institutional research to improve stature? Organizations in which environmental scanning systems have been implemented with some success typically focus the scanning on issues and trends in six broad areas of organizationwide significance: sociocultural, demographic, economic, public policy, political, and technological issues (Hearn and Heydinger 1985). Issues and trends are selectively picked for the most intensive monitoring, and a wide array of information sources are perused as a basis on which to identify trends. Table 7 presents a sample list of issue and trend indicators in the environmental scan along with potential sources of information.

A "scanning team" comprised of topical specialists is designated to examine primary and secondary sources of information for each issue, while a "translation team" comprised of management staff plays an important role in translating the specialists' work through synthesizing and weighting information. The work completed by a number of scanning teams is accumulated by the translation team, synthesized and weighted, and converted into a narrative statement of environmental trends and is-

TABLE 7
ENVIRONMENTAL SCANNING ISSUE AND TREND INDICATORS

Issue/Trend Indicators	Sources of Information
Sociocultural Indicators	
Public confidence in institutions	**National**
Social behavior patterns	Books
Economic attitudes	Public opinion polls
Attitudes toward work, leisure, and education	• Gallup poll
Attitudes toward family, marriage, and childrearing	• News media
Attitudes toward organized religion	• Journal of Public Opinion
Social and ethnic attitudes	• Yankelovich polls/surveys
Attitudes toward environment	• National Opinion Research Center
Attitudes toward profit and non-profit organizations (business and industry, government, labor unions)	• Institute for Social Research
Spending and saving behavior	• Roper surveys
Attitudes toward the military	• Harris surveys
Family structures	Research universities
National, state, and local reports on education	Periodicals
	Retail "fads"

State
Research-teaching universities
News media
Government agencies
Political parties and representatives
Regional organizations (churches, e.g.)
Civic organizations (United Way, e.g.)
Election results

Local
Churches, civic organizations
News media
Elections
County agencies
Social services
Labor organizations
Community action agencies
K–12 school districts

Demographic Indicators	
Population size	**National**
Population characteristics	Census
• Age gradations	Research universities
• Family structures	Departments of Labor and Commerce
• Birth and death rates	

TABLE 7 (continued)

- Income
- Education
- Employment/unemployment
- Handicapping condition
- Minorities
- Male and female
- Work patterns

In-migration/out-migration of population

Enrollment in grades K–12
- High school to college
- Attrition
- Ethnic and racial distribution
- Major field distribution

News media
Research journals
National Institutes of Health and Mental Health
Periodicals
Futurist trend letters
Books
Think tank reports

State
Education associations
Census
Departments of Education, Labor, and Commerce (publications)
Licensing agencies
State offices and agencies
Governor's report
Research-teaching universities
Public and private agencies
Private industry councils
Statewide planning commissions

Local
Census
Regional planning commissions
K–12 school districts

Economic Indicators

Condition of federal and state budgets
Federal deficit
Gross national product
Industrial growth
Capital investment
Labor market
- Growth and decline
- Unemployment
- Underemployment

Inflation
Prime interest rate
Economic development and diversification
Plant closings/attraction of new industry
Structure of labor market
Tax abatement policies of state/local government
Federal taxation policies

National
Departments of Commerce and Labor (publications)
Small Business Administration
News media
Periodicals
Trade journals
Wall Street Journal
Kiplinger Letter
Futurists (Naisbitt trend letter)

State
Departments of Commerce and Labor
Governor's office
Budget office
Legislature
Fiscal agencies
State chamber of commerce
News media
Research universities

TABLE 7 (continued)

Labor union trends
Federal spending policies
Import/export balance
Stock market trends
Investment rates
Foreign investment in economy

Local
News media
State planning agencies
Chamber of commerce
Dodge Report
Annual reports by local businesses
Reports issued by banks and lending institutions
Real estate agencies
Trade organizations (tourism)
College placement data
Surveys of employers
Stock brokerage houses

Public Policy and Political Indicators

Political party platforms (federal and state)
Administrative rule changes
Pending legislation and legislative initiatives
Court rulings
Public speeches
Polls
Election results
Media topics
Executive Orders affecting public agencies
Editorial views in media
Hiring and licensure requirements
Board actions

National
Congressional Record
Federal Register
Court rulings
Trade publications
"Vital" speeches
Newspapers and periodicals
National studies and reports
Television and radio news
Newsletters from representatives

State
State reports
Special commission and task force reports
State agencies
Regional media
Legislative agendas
Newsletters from representatives
Administrative rules
Professional and trade organization newsletters
Labor unions (publications)

Local
News media
Local politicians
Government agencies
Regional planning commissions

TABLE 7 (continued)

Technological Indicators

Trends in energy development resulting from investment in new energy sources, fossil fuels, and energy conservation techniques

Change in educational delivery systems involving advances in computer technology, telecommunications, media systems

Natural resource development in the college service region (energy, minerals, forestry)

Changing technology in information production and retrieval systems

Technological advances that change the composition of the labor force through labor-saving techniques (robotics, advanced computer systems, telecommunications)

Advances in medicine and biological research that improve life expectancy and health

Changing technology leading to the creation of new labor development fields and industrial specializations

Advances in the science of management, business technology, and business communications

National

Trade journals
Research universities
Corporate reports and forecasts
News media
Foundation reports
Conferences and trade shows
Futurists
Associations and societies (publications)
Think tank reports
Federal departments and agencies

State

State agency reports
Governor's reports
State chamber of commerce
Task force and commission reports

Local

News media
Advisory committees
Regional employers
Chamber of commerce
Planning agencies/commissions
Government agencies
Civic associations
Local foundations

sues of relevance to the organization. The narrative statement is typically short, describes issues with immediate and long-term implications, reflects a developing trend, provides information that might not otherwise have reached decision makers' hands, is useful to decision makers, and provides a list and discussion of management options for positioning the organization on the issue.

Perhaps the single most important component of environmental assessment is strategic planning following the narrative statement of environmental trends and issues. Strategic planning is action oriented, concentrating more on the decisions that administrators need to make to align the institution with environmental forces, in contrast to analyses, forecasts, and goals. It especially emphasizes the allocation of resources involving priorities for spending on buildings, equipment, and staff to enable the institution to effectively anticipate or respond to specific conditions in the external environment. Strategic planning is almost surgical in design and effect. After careful analysis and discussion, and using experience and prognoses, administrators decide to cut, amputate, graft, inflate, or strengthen programs and services with infusions of human and financial resources (Keller 1983).

As a practical matter, most colleges and universities will not create an environmental scanning and strategic planning process as complex as that described. Senior officers spend a considerable amount of time trying to understand what is happening in the external environment and sharing reports and observations with one another. The practice is more systematic as part of formally organized strategic planning processes at larger colleges and universities.

Institutional research

Survey research on campus and of constituents' perceptions of institutional goals, operations, and performance is an important tool for enhancing stature. Measures of public opinion of the value of higher education, institutional costs and expenditures, student educational outcomes, and cost effectiveness are important if institutions are to be viewed favorably by the public. Similarly, it is important to conduct research with campus groups—faculty, administrators, students, and classified staff— to determine the extent to which their perceptions of the institution match those of external constituencies. Divergent perceptions can create conflict between expected goals and performance, leading eventually to reduced stature. Convergence of group perceptions achieved through survey research on opinion formation and density can enhance stature by pointing out areas where the college can better align itself with constituents' expectations.

Because little organized research has investigated constituents' perceptions of educational programs and services, colleges and universities need to focus research on gaining detailed information about the attitudes and opinions that internal and external constituencies hold about the college and the effect that

FIGURE 3

CONVERGENCE/DIVERGENCE OF CONSTITUENTS' PERCEPTIONS OF COLLEGE GOALS, COSTS, OPERATIONS, EXPENDITURES, AND PERFORMANCE

College Activity Areas	Constituencies		Convergence/ Divergence
	External	*Internal*	
	Business industry	Faculty	Convergence
		Administrators	Partial conver-
	State agencies	Students	gence
	Community groups	Governing board	Divergence
	Foundations	Classified staff	
	Legislators		
	Regents		
	Private donors		

Institutional goals

Pricing policies (cost)

Operations
  Instruction
  Student services
  General adminis-
    tration
  Plant maintenance
    and operations
  Institutional
    support services
  Academic support
    services
  Research and devel-
    opment

Expenditures

Performance
  Student outcomes
  Institutional out-
    comes
  Value addedness

changes in institutional goals, operations, policies, and performance would have on constituents' attitudes. A simple grid can be developed to show the extent of convergence between internal and external publics (see figure 3).

Management information systems
The assessment tasks mentioned earlier—environmental scanning and measurement of constituents' opinions—lack meaning in the absence of institutional information about costs, resources, outcomes, and performance. Recent studies of institutional information systems give mixed reports; most criticism focuses on the use of information in the decision process (Baldridge, Kemerer, and Green 1982). Every campus should have an effective information system that can be used to determine the institution's capacity for response to forces in the environment. Data managers and decision makers need to learn the procedures that translate data into decisions as part of an overall strategy to enhance stature. Information from an environmental scan, decision processes, and institutional information must be linked to accomplish this goal.

Leveraging Strategies: Allocation of Resources
Institutions facing changes in their external environment that could undermine stature need to build strategies for allocating resources that maximize the institution's responsiveness to external forces. This task can be accomplished using three strategies: (1) evaluation, feedback, and budgeting systems that match institutional resources with identified needs of constituents, (2) timely strategic decisions, and (3) discretionary resources to support innovation.

Timely decisions through integrated evaluation
and budgeting systems
Many institutions continue to allocate resources as an increment or decrement over the previous year's budget without regard for important program and service changes that must be made to respond to external forces. An absolutely essential ingredient for stature in a context of growing criticism is information about forces in the external environment and the effectiveness of current programs and services in addressing those forces. To illustrate, information about the labor market's changing needs for knowledge and technical skills in the professions, when matched with data describing program performance in producing graduates with those skills, adds an important dimension to the process of allocating resources. This information can provide a road map for an institution to identify programs that contribute to or detract from stature and a way of directing the necessary resources for making changes. Institutions that are

able to merge fully developed environmental scanning and program review systems with the budgetary process will be able to enhance stature through timely decisions directing the flow of resources to highly visible activities.

College staff exhibit a natural reluctance to change existing approaches to allocating resources unless the benefits of doing so can be demonstrated. This reluctance stems not from a negative outlook but from inner psychological needs for control, expedience, and predictability in the budgetary process. Such internal forces of resistance diminish stature by retarding institutional response to conditions in the external environment. They can be overcome if a future-oriented, participative approach to budgeting is implemented. This approach provides a similar starting point for all staff and uses the participants' feelings about future prospects for the institution as part of the initial data base for financial projections. The futuring process helps to swing participants' focus from resistance to change to planning for a desirable future state that benefits both the institution and the individual. Instead of being a forum for petty complaints, the budgetary process should serve as a rallying point for determination of what the institution must do to upgrade its stature. Instead of simply allocating resources, future-oriented, participative budgeting can contribute to the formulation of strong statements about institutional weaknesses and encourage staff to look beyond their departments to see institutional issues.

Instead of being a forum for petty complaints, the budgetary process should serve as a rallying point for determination of what the institution must do to upgrade its stature.

Support for innovation

How can an institution make major changes in its programs and services to build stature if it does not have discretionary resources to support innovation? Consider, for example, the cumulative effects of reduction experienced by institutions in the late 1970s and early 1980s that are still being felt today:

- Real declines in resources (even in wealthy institutions) as great as 20 percent of academic budgets;
- Cumulative deficits in expenditures for equipment, repair of the physical plant, and even salaries that collectively may have been as great as another 10 or 20 percent of academic budgets;
- Rising costs in some sectors of college and university expenditures, such as energy, computing, and libraries, that

consume all or most of the budgetary flexibility that institutions generate, and more;

- A projected demographic decline of as much as 20 or 30 percent in the traditional college-age population that will—to what degree administrators do not know—negatively affect enrollments and therefore the resource base;
- The lowest rate of faculty turnover and therefore internal budgetary flexibility that colleges have known in over 30 years;
- Decreasing opportunities for professional development and therefore decreasing attractiveness of academic careers for new junior faculty in many sectors of the institution; and superimposed on all of these effects
- Prolonged duration of the problem, continuing from nearly a decade in the past to perhaps a decade into the future, that precludes temporizing and bridging solutions and creates the discouraging sense that the necessity to manage these sorts of problems will foreclose any constructive and significant efforts to enhance stature (Frye 1984).

How, in short, do faculty and administrators talk meaningfully about innovation when institutions at the present time typically have considerably less than 1 percent of their annual budgets available to put into real program development?

If colleges and universities expect to build stature through innovation, they will need substantial discretionary resources, which can be accomplished through three methods. First, a "change by substitution" strategy can be employed in which marginal programs are pared back (or eliminated) and the resulting "savings" applied to innovation. Second, new resources can be sought at the institution and department levels based on a clear-cut understanding that whatever monies are collected will be applied to innovation. Private gifts and donations are the most likely source of new money. Because effective fund-raising systems take years to build, institutions should not expect an immediate influx of resources for innovation using this method. Third, an annual "tax" can be applied to the budgets of academic and nonacademic departments to produce discretionary income. Working as a forced contingency approach to the development of resources, the effect over time will be to increase the percentage of the operating budget available for innovation.

The array and quality of programs available to meet emerging needs is a critical factor affecting the way in which important constituencies view the institution. The lack of resources to support innovation could be the greatest impediment to colleges' and universities' efforts to enhance stature in the 1990s.

Leveraging Strategies: Outcomes Assessment

During the past five years, a movement has gained momentum to gauge institutional effectiveness and to justify public support for higher education by evaluating the outcomes and benefits produced by individual institutions. Elected officials, coordinating boards, state government agencies, and accrediting associations have shifted away from the traditional benchmarks of quality (for example, ratio of accepted to rejected applicants, admission scores of entering students, number of books in the library, size of endowment and physical plant, credentials of faculty, expenditures per student) to greater emphasis upon the products or outcomes of education. The impetus exists to link stature to outcomes:

Colleges must begin to assess their performance and publish the results, because parents and students are growing uneasy about the rapid rise in tuition costs and they need consumer protection. Because colleges have not provided such information, the rumor mill has flourished and prospective students face a landscape barren of real information with which to make informed choices, but littered instead with trendy indicators of campus popularity and status. No one wants high school seniors depending on slick publications that claim to tell it like it really is. The traditional gauges of academic quality—input measures such as faculty-student ratios, the number of students with doctorates, and library holdings— bear little on what critics charge are academe's shortcomings: that many of our graduates do not seem to possess the knowledge, skills, and in some cases the character and civic virtues that should constitute a highly educated person. Virtually nobody, at least nobody outside the academy, believes the resources are lacking. The case can be made that the American people have been ungenerous to higher education. They have not and we all know that. To address their problems, colleges and universities must focus not on inputs but on the quality of teaching and curricular reform. They should state their goals and make the results available to everyone. Institutions should employ a variety of evaluation methods, including standardized tests, interviews and questionnaires, reviews of students' written work and extracurricular activities, and studies of alumni and dropouts (Bennett 1985).

Comprehensive outcomes assessment
The link between quality and outcomes has obvious implications for stature in colleges and universities. Repeated documentation of institutional performance in producing college graduates with exceptional general education and competencies in their major field using widely recognized indicators will encourage public recognition of stature for a specific institution. One question must be answered: What outcomes assessment strategy(ies) should an institution select for the purpose of enhancing stature from a range of potential strategies that can be used? Stated in the lexicon of administrators: What strategy will yield the greatest benefits (stature) at the lowest cost (time and efficiency)?

Institutions accomplish different goals through outcomes assessment, each goal requiring a different assessment strategy and having different implications for enhancing stature. The variation in assessment goals includes (1) measuring the effectiveness of remedial/developmental curricula toward improving the basic skills of lower-division students; (2) ensuring that each student has developed the expected basic skills by the time he or she reaches the junior year in college; (3) measuring the effectiveness of the undergraduate core curricula and co-curricular programs toward developing the general education knowledge and skills as well as the affective development expected of college graduates; (4) measuring the effectiveness of academic programs in developing the knowledge and skills of graduating seniors in their major fields of study; and (5) assuring the public that each college graduate has the general education and competence in a major field expected of college graduates (Nettles 1987).

Each of these assessment goals not only requires a different approach but also produces a different set of consequences. For example, the goal of measuring the effectiveness of remedial/developmental curricula toward improving the basic skills of lower-division students embodies an underlying assumption (of the general public) that students receiving a college education should be able to read, to write, and to perform basic mathematical calculations. As such, stature is not likely to be significantly enhanced through a strategy focused on documenting the college's performance in providing students with something that is already expected—proficiency in basic skills. On the other hand, advances in stature are apt to be forthcoming through published information depicting the effectiveness of colleges in developing general education and competence in major fields that enable individuals to contribute to society. Measurement of near-term and long-term student outcomes in work, further education, and community is a science that is in an embryonic stage of development. Faculty and administrators are just now learning what indicators and methods to use to measure outcomes. Therefore, institutions with a capacity to produce and publicize information describing near-term and long-term student outcomes using an array of measures will be able to exert considerable leverage in enhancing stature compared to institutions without this capacity.

Institutions choosing to undertake comprehensive assessment of student outcomes as a method to enhance stature should routinely collect the following types of information from students:

Near-term outcomes (one to three years after college enrollment):
- Relationship of job to curriculum directly after college attendance
- Personal income immediately after college attendance
- Enrollment in advanced degree programs
- Assessment of cognitive learning and skill development upon exit from college
- Performance of graduates on tests in major fields of study
- Students' performance on tests required for admission to graduate school (GRE, GMAT, LSAT, for example)
- Students' GPA in advanced degree programs
- Honors or awards received by students in work or education
- Employers' assessments of students' job performance one to three years after college attendance
- Service to the community one to three years after college attendance (memberships in civic organizations, elected office, volunteer work, and so on)

Long-term outcomes (four to ten years after college enrollment):
- Advanced degrees earned

- Personal income and salary mobility
- Property ownership
- Job mobility and promotions
- Supervisory responsibility
- Honors and awards
- Employer's assessment of employee's performance and value to the organization
- Leadership positions in local, state, and national organizations
- Service to the community
- Service to the state and nation
- Improvement in the quality of life (Alfred 1987).

The extent to which outcomes assessment is a viable tool for enhancing stature depends on the college's mission and on certain characteristics of key constituencies. Many institutions serve constituencies with specific needs and expectations, which determine the way in which information about outcomes is viewed and reported. And because constituents' needs are apt to change rapidly in the future as societal conditions change, the notion of what is "desirable" and what is "undesirable" in outcomes may also change. Colleges and universities will need to carefully monitor the relationship between societal conditions and public opinion if they are to make meaningful judgments about what type(s) of information about student outcomes to use in enhancing stature.

Beneficiaries' satisfaction

College faculty and administrators need to know more about the perceptions that different groups hold of the college experience. Students benefit directly from exposure to academic programs and services. They possess a wealth of knowledge about the "process" side of teaching and learning that can be used to improve educational outcomes. Business and industry executives, government officials, and civic leaders receive the "products" of higher education and are indirect beneficiaries of teaching and learning. They can help by providing information about the relationship between education and work, education and citizenship, and education and quality of life.

How can institutions enhance stature through knowledge they have about beneficiaries' perceptions? First, they can develop assessment instruments that elicit information from specific groups about the effects of teaching and instruction. Is instruction relevant to the job? Does it provide access for students to entry-level and advanced positions in a labor market undergoing structural change? Does it prepare students for success in advanced degree programs? Does it facilitate occupational success through access to technology and cultivation of higher-order thinking skills? Does it lead to improvement in the quality of life through competence in general education? Does it improve health, family life, use of leisure time, and social skills through heightened awareness? Does it improve the capacity of individuals to adapt to rapid change by cultivating important skills (flexibility, intellectual curiosity, openness to change, problem-solving ability)? Does it facilitate interest in public service leading to social and economic development of local communities?

Second, they can convert the results of assessment into decisions aimed at improving instruction and support services. When evidence is found of beneficiaries' dissatisfaction and less-than-desirable outcomes, needed changes can be identified and implemented, thereby demonstrating a commitment on the part of the institution to client service. An orientation toward client service is an important feature of the efforts of business and industry to enhance stature, and it has value for higher education as well.

Cost management

Colleges and universities are selling highly intangible products with associated tangible costs. The college student pays greatly in terms of time, money, loss of other potential income, psychic costs, and inconvenience. College attendance calls for an extreme level of involvement from the consumer. For a college to maintain stature in the eyes of consumers, costs must fall into line with the perceived benefits of education. To ensure an appropriate balance between costs and benefits, colleges and universities need to undertake research on the psychic costs of college attendance among current and potential students, parents, and others who pay tuition. To do so would involve assessment, using survey and interview techniques, of the levels at which individual perceptions of price exceed those of the benefits received or, in the lexicon of marketing specialists, the point at which an uneven exchange occurs between the institution and the consumer.

Marketing strategies should be carefully developed to clarify costs to the consumer, the predictable benefits of attendance at

a particular college, and basic elements of the relationship between benefits and costs (total dollars spent on education and average rates of return on investment). Seminars should be organized for parents, high school counselors, and education journalists in which institutional officials explain pricing policies. Easily understood communication techniques, including jargon-free verbal presentations, animated videos, and student profile descriptions, should be used to ensure attendees fully understand the complex topic.

Leveraging Strategies: Image Management
A distinction has been made between stature and related concepts of image, reputation, and quality. The image of an institution, however, is part of its day-to-day reality in dealings with the general public. It is an institution's image, not necessarily its identity, that constituencies respond to. A not uncommon expression among college and university administrators is that "perception is reality." An institution's actual quality is often less important than its prestige, or reputation for quality. Perceptions are critical, for quality and prestige do not always move hand in hand (Huddleston and Karr 1982; Walters and Paul 1970).

Public affairs is the dimension of management in colleges and universities responsible for advancing an image of the institution to the public. Many elements, including outreach materials, media communications, and physical environment, contribute to an institution's image. Administrators, faculty, and staff should be concerned about their institution's image and how it contributes to stature for three reasons:

1. They need to know how their institution is perceived in relationship to competing institutions.
2. They need to know how the institution is perceived in terms of its capacity to respond to emerging societal forces by those who contribute resources.
3. They need to know how the institution is perceived by their various audiences—students, alumni, potential donors, and business and industry executives.

Without a doubt, prevailing images of colleges and universities held by multiple publics affect stature. The question, however, is not whether postsecondary institutions using aggressive techniques of public relations should improve stature at the expense of other institutions. The real question is what colleges and universities can do through management of public affairs to improve the stature of higher education as a total enterprise while at the same time leveraging the stature of local institutions.

Image profile

College and university administrators interested in using imaging techniques as a method to enhance stature should focus on knowing (1) the substance of information that publics see, hear, and read about the institution, (2) the beliefs, attitudes, and perceptions that publics hold in relation to the college as a whole or as a sum of parts, and (3) the effectiveness of public affairs in eliciting desirable images. A college's image can be described as an organized set of beliefs that people associate with the institution. These beliefs tend to be oversimplified notions about qualities such as academic reputation, faculty expertise, athletic emphasis, or campus appearance. Image beliefs are formed as individuals gain information about a college through the media, interpersonal exchanges, and direct experience. Thus, college image represents how people perceive an institution but does not necessarily reflect the true nature of the college (Huddleston and Karr 1982).

The importance of college image has been overlooked (Fram 1982). College administrators have focused on techniques for recruiting and retaining students but have ignored the broader issue of maintaining and enhancing an image for a specific college that is based upon constituents' perceptions of the institution's key attributes. For example, a hypothetical college might be perceived as having a competitive academic environment, an emphasis on athletic programs, and an impersonal atmosphere. Although an image of a college may not be accurate, it may serve as the basis on which individuals make judgments about the stature of the institution.

College administrators need to assess institutional image among relevant constituencies if they expect to understand important dynamics underlying stature. Relevant attributes to be considered include campus environment, research activity by faculty, quality of teaching, and pricing. Once college image has been assessed, administrators are then in a position to maintain and strengthen the positive aspects of image and to improve negative or weak aspects.

Although the rationale for assessing college image is clear, the methodology for measuring this concept is not well developed. A review of the literature shows few studies in which the overall image of an institution has been measured. Most research on the public's attitudes toward colleges and universities can be classified as "opinion surveys." That is, a sample of subjects are asked to state their preferences or expectations for institutional roles, programs, and policies (Biggs et al. 1975; Haskins 1975; Owings 1977).

In some studies, subjects are asked how they perceive a college attribute such as registration procedures or university-community relations (Jameson et al. 1973; Rossman 1975). Such studies measure only a single facet of college image, however.

A promising approach to the assessment of college image suggested for administrators interested in improving stature is the image profile technique of Huddleston and Karr (1982). Image can be measured as a multidimensional concept by having constituencies rate the college on a series of semantic differential scales anchored by bipolar traits like "superior academic reputation" and "inferior academic reputation." Average scores for the constituency can then be plotted across the series of scales in such a way that an "image profile" is revealed.

Determination of an image profile is useful in many respects. Foremost, the profile is a visually concise description of how the public perceives numerous attributes of the college. The profile of a college can easily be compared to image profiles generated for other competing institutions or an "ideal institution." In addition, several groups can complete image profiles for a single institution and the similarities and differences between groups' perceptions compared.

Capacity for distinctiveness
All too often, college administrators respond to problems of image and visibility by developing new publications or throwing more money into the public relations budget to communicate a generalized institutional image. Or they adopt techniques to enhance image that have been successfully implemented on other campuses without careful consideration of special characteristics of their own campus that may facilitate or impede success (Hilpert and Alfred 1987). College administrators seeking to improve institutional image, and ultimately stature, need to determine which elements of institutional uniqueness can be

communicated to the public and whether institutional publications, events, and news releases support these elements.

For example, if the institution's primary claim to distinctiveness receives expression in the characteristics of an "intellectual community," it is important that imaging activities be based on applied research that demonstrates what the term "intellectual" means to 18-year-olds and other groups. Methods then need to be devised to represent the concept of uniqueness in terms meaningful to specific target audiences. Public affairs specialists engaged in the imaging of institutional distinctiveness to specific constituencies need to ask certain questions:

- What specific factors contribute to the uniqueness of the institution?
- How do curricular programs, institutional policies, and support services relate to uniqueness?
- How do institutional publications, events, news releases, faculty and staff attitudes, and the leader's persona and behavior contribute to the concept of distinctiveness? Do they adequately communicate the concept to target audiences?
- What actions can be taken to improve the public's perception of institutional uniqueness in ways that benefit the institution?

Opinion management

As institutions become aware of the role that image plays in enhancing stature, they will begin to reevaluate their relationships with specific constituencies. They will become more selective about the publics they attempt to reach, and they will seek to influence the opinions held by important publics. Specific criteria will be established for defining which publics are important as well as the range and types of opinions that the college wants these publics to formulate and maintain.

Implementation of a program of special events and activities designed to cultivate favorable opinions among specific constituencies will be essential if colleges are to elevate stature. Essentially, this strategy relates to increasing personal contact with groups and individuals whose support is important to the college. An effective opinion management program should have well-defined short-term goals and employ the most effective contact method. For example, college officials seeking to build relationships with regional high school counselors for the purpose of eliciting favorable opinions (about the institution) could provide feedback loops to regional high schools, informing high school counselors of their graduates' achievements at the institution. Several additional steps also need to be taken to manage constituencies' opinions:

- Study the values, attitudes, and interests of specific constituency groups in relation to complex organizations in general and higher education in particular. Voting records, speeches, newspaper and magazine articles, gifts and donations, and public opinion surveys are good sources to accomplish this task.
- Involve college personnel in seminars and workshops to discuss the objectives of opinion management and the strategies to be employed with specific groups based on research information.
- Put together a strategy complete with target groups, activities, opinion priorities, timetables, and accountability for opinion management.
- Foster strong working relationships with public- and private-sector organizations that can assist the college in getting its message across to target groups.

Once college staff have established credible relationships with key individuals and target groups using these steps, opinion management will be easier. Staff will be communicating from a position of strength, and target groups will know that their interests are being addressed through institutional programs, policies, and services.

Crisis communication management

Recent events have brought about a growing awareness of the need for colleges and universities to develop capabilities for crisis communication management (Morrell 1987). The corporate world has faced tampering with Tylenol, the accidents at Three Mile Island and Chernobyl, the attempted assassination of President Reagan, and the chemical release in Bhopal, India. Experience has shown that some of the best-managed companies in America have not been fully prepared to deal with problems that often strike quickly. Colleges and universities should take heed as well.

The failure of a college or university to plan for crisis and to communicate with the public so as to safeguard institutional image and interests can have severe repercussions. The institution could suffer a temporary public relations setback with a limited number of constituencies or a crippling blow to stature with the general public. Consider, for example, the public relations consequences that an institution without a crisis communication plan would face if AIDS were discovered among several students on campus. Drug abuse and its consequences pose constant threats. Colleges and universities are managed on a much more decentralized basis than private industry and lines of authority less clearly drawn, making it particularly difficult for academic institutions to respond to a crisis quickly and effectively.

How can college and university administrators safeguard institutional image in periods of crisis? First, a crisis committee should be appointed, consisting of senior administrators who can be called together on short notice (Morrell 1987). Various campus constituencies should be represented on the committee to provide broad expertise and to ensure better communication. Second, a crisis communication plan should be developed and a spokesperson designated for the institution. A related policy decision concerns the degree to which the institution is willing to share information with the press and public. In this regard, the college or university must balance the need to protect individuals, and to some extent the integrity of the institution, with the campus's and the public's right to know. In a number of situations, educational institutions have released a minimum of information to the press only to have a newspaper conduct its own investigation of the incident and publish a detailed article, placing the institution in an awkward position with a public relations problem. Withholding information also fuels the rumor mill; the tragedies in private industry have taught administrators that full disclosure is generally the best policy.

The crisis communication plan should contain general guidelines for coping with particular situations. For example, if a dormitory cannot be used because of structural problems, some provision might be made to have construction experts provide information to the public about methods the college will use to resolve the problem. Taking these steps and being prepared for a crisis give an institution distinct advantages. It provides a guide for action when handling a campus crisis, minimizes possible further damage to individuals and campus reputation, demonstrates that the institution is prepared to act prudently concerning events that cannot be anticipated, and safeguards the institution against loss of stature.

SUMMARY AND CONCLUSIONS

Although most recent surveys of public attitudes evidence a positive disposition toward higher education, colleges and universities are encountering major signs of discontent. Concerns about rapid increases in tuition costs, scandals in college athletics, the quality of faculty and academic programs, the unfair use of tax-exempt status to operate money-making activities, employers' dissatisfaction with the knowledge and technical skills of graduates, intensified competition for students and resources, and poorly documented relationships between the costs and benefits of college attendance permeate the media. Colleges and universities are resource-acquiring institutions. They understand that positive public attitudes toward their goals, programs, and performance are important because they affect their financial stability and support. Given this reality, higher education institutions have no choice but to be cognizant of their stature with important constituencies if they expect to gain and hold public support.

Institutional stature is comprised of two related but unidentical components— "satisfaction" and "affect."

Stature may be understood as the totality of perceptions and representations held by specific individuals, groups, and publics in reference to particular characteristics and/or performance attributes projected by colleges and universities over time. Its forms of expression in colleges and universities and the contexts in which it can be viewed (macro and micro) are multiple. The central or integrating focus for stature across all institutions is the relationship of the institution to its external environment as seen through the eyes of important constituencies. Implicit in this relationship are multiple points of contact between the institution and the environment that comprise the dimensions of stature. These dimensions relate to societal forces, the needs and expectations of constituencies, and attributes and characteristics of the academic organization.

As societal forces and public opinion toward social institutions have changed, transition has occurred in the stature of colleges and universities. At least five facts seem clear:

- Public confidence in the leaders of social institutions and in major educational institutions like colleges and universities declined without interruption between 1966 and 1984.
- Individuals and groups react to colleges and universities as they see them not as they objectively are. Perceptions of institutional stature are influenced by the values, expectations, experience, and personality traits individuals bring to the situation.

- Institutional stature is comprised of two related but uni-dentical components—"satisfaction" and "affect." Opinions expressed by important constituencies in relationship to specific attributes of a college or university are an aspect of positive or negative "affect" that influences stature.
- "Satisfaction" is a function of the gap an individual perceives between prevailing societal conditions, his or her needs and expectations, and college performance in producing benefits that satisfy needs. Changes in the level of satisfaction may result from change in societal conditions, change in individual needs and expectations, change in institutional performance, or all three. The degree and direction of change determine perceptions held by the individual of institutional stature.
- "Satisfaction" and "affect" are necessary preconditions for stature. The absence of either condition serves to constrain stature in colleges and universities. The absence of both conditions will effectively negate the perception of stature.

Attributes of the academic organization in colleges and universities, such as good ambiguity, disciplinary organization, inactivity and insulation of staff, and professional autonomy, resist change and retard the capacity of institutions to improve stature. Academic programs, services, and staff are fixed resources and change slowly. The domains of activity pursued by faculty and administrators do not necessarily reflect common goals, nor do they center exclusively on the satisfaction of public expectations. A professional staff, acting on the basis of limited comprehension of the external environment in a loosely coupled organization, engenders performance outputs that do not always satisfy identified needs. The effect of this circumstance is to magnify the effort required of administrators in scanning the environment to determine how the institution must alter programs, services, and staff to meet constituents' needs.

Institutions may be prepared to respond to changing public perceptions and expectations through adjustments in the informal organization (for example, establishment of nontraditional delivery systems) but not to give them sanction in the formal organization. In colleges and universities with traditional prestige (for example, Harvard and Princeton) low correlation may exist between public expectations and the structure and operations of the academic organization.

Practices to enhance stature in complex organizations focus on assessment of elements in the external environment that are not easily controlled, such as social forces, public attitudes, and the behavior of consumers. In colleges and universities, the focus is on elements internal to the organization that can be more easily controlled—institutional publications, communication and public relations, outreach, involvement in campus activities, and campus-based performance assessment. A few institutions have grasped the importance of institutional stature and—borrowing from successful practices in complex organizations—have designed and implemented strategies to improve it. The majority, however, concentrate on short-term marketing practices that rely solely on communication.

Colleges and universities are not doing all they can to enhance stature through current organizational practices. Until faculty and administrators address underlying management problems related to strategic assessment, allocation of resources, outcomes assessment, and image management, leveraging strategies for enhancing stature will not be effective in higher education institutions.

REFERENCES

The Educational Resources Information Center (ERIC) Clearinghouse
on Higher Education abstracts and indexes the current literature on
higher education for inclusion in ERIC's data base and announcement
in ERIC's monthly bibliographic journal, *Resources in Education*
(RIE). Most of these publications are available through the ERIC
Document Reproduction Service (EDRS). For publications cited in this
bibliography that are available from EDRS, ordering number and price
are included. Readers who wish to order a publication should write to
the ERIC Document Reproduction Service, 3900 Wheeler Avenue,
Alexandria, Virginia 22304. (Phone orders with VISA or MasterCard
are taken at 800/227–ERIC or 703/823–0500.) When ordering, please
specify the document (ED) number. Documents are available as noted
in microfiche (MF) and paper copy (PC). Because prices are subject to
change, it is advisable to check the latest issue of *Resources in
Education* for current cost based on the number of pages in the
publication.

Alfred, Richard. 1987. "Defining Effectiveness through Student
  Outcomes Assessment." In *Academic Effectiveness: Transforming
  Colleges and Universities,* edited by Michael Waggoner, Richard
  Alfred, Marlene Francis, and Marvin Peterson. Ann Arbor:
  University of Michigan.
Astin, Alexander. 1982. "Why Not Try Some New Ways of
  Measuring Quality?" *Educational Record* 63(2): 10–15.
Astin, Alexander, and Solmon, Lewis. 1979. "Measuring Academic
  Quality: An Interim Report." *Change* 11(6): 48–51.
Astin, Alexander, et al. 1985. *The American Freshman: National
  Norms for Fall 1984.* Los Angeles: Cooperative Institutional
  Research Program of the American Council on Education and the
  University of California. ED 255 106. 193 pp. MF–$1.07; PC not
  available EDRS.
Baldridge, J. Victor. 1971. "Environmental Pressure, Professional
  Autonomy, and Coping Strategies in Academic Organizations." In
  Academic Governance, edited by J. V. Baldridge. Berkeley, Cal.:
  McCutchan.
———. March/April 1980. "Managerial Rules for Successful
  Implementation." *Journal of Higher Education* 51: 117–34.
Baldridge, J. Victor; Curtis, David; Ecker, George; and Riley, Gary.
  1978. *Policy Making and Effective Leadership.* San Francisco:
  Jossey-Bass.
Baldridge, J. Victor; Kemerer, Frank; and Green, Kenneth. 1982. *The
  Enrollment Crisis: Factors, Actors, and Impacts.* AAHE-ERIC
  Higher Education Report No. 3. Washington, D.C.: American
  Association for Higher Education. ED 222 158. 79 pp. MF–$1.07;
  PC–$10.03.
Barnes, S., and Inglehart, P. 1974. "Affluence, Individual Values,

and Social Change." In *Subjective Elements of Well-Being*, edited
by B. Stumpel. Paris: Organization for Economic Cooperation and
Development.

Barthell, Frank. 1984. "A Medley of Radio Winners." *CASE
Currents* 10(3): 23.

Behar, Richard. 1985. "Cleaning Up?" *Forbes* 135(6): 94–98.

Bennett, W.J. 28 October 1985. An address (untitled) presented to the
American Council on Education at the Fountaine Bleau Hotel.

Berger, L., and Luckmann, T. 1966. *The Social Construction of
Reality: A Treatise in the Sociology of Knowledge*. New York:
Doubleday & Co.

Bers, Trudy. 1985. "Marketing Economic Development and
Institutional Research." Paper presented at AIR Conference,
Portland, Oregon, April.

Biggs, Donald, et al. 1975. *Citizens' Attitudes toward the University
of Minnesota*. Research Bulletin 15(13). Minneapolis: University of
Minnesota.

Borgen, Joseph, and Shade, William. 1984. "Joining Others for
Community Economic Development." In *New Directions for
Community Colleges* No. 12. San Francisco: Jossey-Bass.

Brouillette, John, and Rogers, David. 1980. *Higher Education in
Colorado: The Citizens' Viewpoint*. Fort Collins: Colorado State
University, Department of Sociology. ED 197 683. 192 pp. MF–
$1.07; PC–$18.30.

Buck, Douglas. 1984. "A Medley of Radio Winners." *CASE
Currents* 10(3): 21.

Burns, J. M. 1978. *Leadership*. New York: Harper & Row.

Business Week. 16 August 1985. "Two Weary Innkeepers Try to
Renovate."

Cameron, Kim. 1978. "Measuring Organizational Effectiveness in
Institutions of Higher Education." *Administrative Science Quarterly*
23: 604–32.

Campbell, Angus. 1981. *The Sense of Well-Being in America*. New
York: McGraw-Hill.

Campbell, Angus; Converse, Philip; and Rogers, W. 1976. *The
Quality of American Life*. New York: Russell Sage Foundation.

Chakravoty, Subrata. 1985. "Thank You, Bill Agee." *Forbes* 135(5):
44–48.

Chickering, Arthur. 1981. *The Modern American College: Responding
to the New Realities of Diverse Students and a Changing Society*.
San Francisco: Jossey-Bass.

Clark, Burton. 1983. *The Higher Education System: Academic
Organization in Cross-National Perspective*. Berkeley: University of
California Press.

Cleveland, Harlan. 1980. *Renewing the Boundless Resource* (Summary

of 1949 quotation in national Higher Education Report, p. 2),
Kellogg Lecture presented at the AASCU Annual Meeting, San
Antonio, Texas, 1979.

Cohen, Michael, and March, James. 1974. *Leadership and Ambiguity:
The American College President*. New York: McGraw-Hill.

Congressional Quarterly Almanac. 1973. Washington, D.C.:
Congressional Quarterly.

Cope, Robert. 1981. "Environmental Assessments for Strategic
Planning." In *New Directions for Institutional Research* No. 31.
San Francisco: Jossey-Bass.

Couretas, John. 1985. "Preparing for the Worst." *Business Marketing*
70(11): 96–100.

Coury, John. 1984. "AMA Activities Related to the Public Image of
Physicians." *Report of the Board of Trustees of the American
Medical Association*.

Crockett, David. 1984. "A Medley of Radio Winners." *CASE
Currents* 10(3): 18.

D'Agostino, Joseph. 1985. "It's Academic." *CASE Currents* 11(9).

Davies, John, and Melchiori, Gerlinda. 1982. "Developing the Image
and Public Reputation of Universities: The Managerial Process."
*International Journal of Institutional Management in Higher
Education* 6(2): 87–108.

Davis, William. 1986. "Strengthening a Partnership with the State."
CASE Currents 12(2).

de l'Ain, Bertrand. 1981. "Certifying Effect and Consumer Effect:
Some Remarks on Strategies Employed by Higher Education
Institutions." *Higher Education* 10(1): 55–71.

Diefenbach, John. August 1983. "What's in a Corporate Identity? A
Lot, So Don't Change It Carelessly." *American Banker* 148: 10–
12.

Dill, David. 1982. "The Management of Academic Culture: Notes on
the Management of Meaning and Social Integration." *Higher
Education* 11: 303–20.

Dowling, J., and Pfeffer, Jeffrey. 1975. "Organizational Legitimacy,
Social Values, and Organizational Behavior." *Pacific Sociological
Review* 18(1): 122–36.

Doyle, P., and Newbould, G. D. 1980. "A Strategic Approach to
Marketing a University." *Journal of Educational Administration*
18(2): 254–70. Also in Ryans, C. C., and Shanklin, W. L., eds.
*Strategic Planning, Marketing, and Public Relations and Fund-
Raising in Higher Education: Perspectives, Readings, and
Annotated Bibliography*. Metuchen, N.J.: Scarecrow Press.

Drucker, Peter. 1973. *Management: Tasks, Responsibilities, Practices*.
New York: Harper & Row.

Elton, Scott. 1984. "A Medley of Radio Winners." *CASE Currents*
10(3): 20.

Ewell, Peter. 1987. "Transformational Leadership for Improving Student Outcomes." In *Academic Effectiveness: Transforming Colleges and Universities*, edited by Michael Waggoner, Richard Alfred, Marlene Francis, and Marvin Peterson. Ann Arbor: University of Michigan.

Fisher, Anne. 1983. "Peering Past Pepsico's Bad News." *Fortune* 108(10): 124–33.

Folger, John. 1980. "Implications of State Government Changes." In *Improving Academic Management: A Handbook of Planning and Institutional Research*, edited by Paul Jedamus and Marvin Peterson. San Francisco: Jossey-Bass.

Fram, Eugene. 1982. "Maintaining and Enhancing a College or University Image." Paper presented at AIR conference, Denver, Colorado, May. ED 220 044. 22 pp. MF–$1.07; PC–$3.85.

Frye, William. 1984. "Observations on Academic Renewal." In *Academic Renewal: Advancing Higher Education toward the Nineties*, edited by Michael Waggoner, Richard Alfred, and Marvin Peterson. Ann Arbor, Mich.: School of Education.

Gallup Organization. 1985. *Public Opinion Survey: Attitudes toward Higher Education*. Princeton, N.J.: Author.

Gilbert, Heather. 1985. "Keep 'em Learning." *CASE Currents* 11(6): 42–43.

Grunde, Andris. Winter 1976. "Self-Selection and Institutional Images in College Admissions." *NASPA Journal* 13: 21–24.

Halsey, Mary. 1985. "What Parents Want." *CASE Currents* 11(6): 10–13.

Hample, Stephen. 1985. "Using Television to Report Institutional Research Findings." Paper presented at AIR conference, Portland, Oregon, April.

Haskins, J. June 1975. "Tennesseean's Opinions toward Higher Education and the University of Tennessee." *Statewide Opinion Survey.* Preliminary Report No. One. Knoxville: University of Tennessee, College of Communication. ED 134 092. 39 pp. MF–$1.07; PC–$5.79.

Hearn, James, and Heydinger, Richard. 1985. "Scanning the University's External Environment." *Journal of Higher Education* 56(4): 429–45.

Hechinger, Fred. Winter 1977. "The Public Perception of Higher Education." *College Board Review* 102: 5–12.

Hessenflow, Louise. 1985. "Imaging and Marketing Health Care Organizations and Professions." Unpublished paper. Raleigh, N.C.

Hilpert, John, and Alfred, Richard. 1987. "Improving Enrollment Success: Presidents Hold the Key." *Educational Record* 68(3): 30–35.

Holmes, Terry; Miller, Elise; and Varon, Jerome. 1985. "Family Affair." *CASE Currents* 11(6): 20–23.

Hooper, Mark. 1984. "The Alumni Lobby." *CASE Currents* 11(7): 36–39.

Huddleston, T., and Karr, M. 1982. "Assessing College Image." *College and University* 57(4): 364–70.

Hutton, Cynthia. 1986. "America's Most Admired Corporations." *Fortune* 113(1): 16–22.

Hyland, John. 1984. "Working with Communities as Centers of Special Interest Groups." In *New Directions for Community Colleges* No. 12. San Francisco: Jossey-Bass.

Jameson, B., et al. 1973. "The General Public Views the University: A Report of Community Interviews." Washington, D.C.: Office of Education, Division of Higher Education Research.

Johnson, Terry, and Smith, Vern. 27 July 1987. "What's Wrong with Delta?" *Newsweek*: 25.

Jones, Richard. 1984. "Supplement Your Coverage." *CASE Currents* 11(7): 40–42.

Kalisch, Philip, and Kalisch, Beatrice. August 1980. "Perspectives on Improving Nursing's Public Image." *Nursing and Healthcare*: 10–15.

————. January 1983. "Improving the Image of Nursing." *American Journal of Nursing*: 48–54.

Kalisch, Philip; Kalisch, Beatrice; and Clinton, Jacqueline. 1982. "The World of Nursing and Prime-time Television, 1950–1980." *Nursing Research* 31(6): 358–63.

Katz, Daniel, and Kahn, Robert. 1978. *The Social Psychology of Organizations*. 2d ed. New York: John Wiley & Sons.

Keller, George. 1983. *Academic Strategy: The Management Revolution in American Higher Education*. Baltimore: Johns Hopkins University Press.

Kleiman, Michael, and Clemente, Frank. 1976. "Public Confidence in Educational Leaders." *Intellect* 105(2379): 161–62.

Kotler, Philip, and Fox, Karen. 1985. *Strategic Marketing for Educational Institutions*. Englewood Cliffs, N.J.: Prentice-Hall.

Kotler, P., and Levy, S.J. 1978. "Broadening the Concept of Marketing." In *Marketing in Nonprofit Organizations,* edited by P.J. Montana. New York: AMACOM, 1978. Also in Kotler, P.; Ferrell, O. C.; and Lamb, C., eds. *Cases and Readings for Marketing for Nonprofit Organizations.* Englewood Cliffs, N.J.: Prentice-Hall, 1983.

Kraushaar, Steven. 1984. "A Medley of Radio Winners." *CASE Currents* 10(3): 20.

Kuh, George. 1981. *Indices of Quality in Undergraduate Education*. AAHE-ERIC Higher Education Report No. 4. Washington, D.C.: American Association for Higher Education. ED 213 340. 50 pp. MF–$1.07; PC–$5.79.

Lane, R. 1978. "Markets and the Satisfaction of Human Wants." *Journal of Economic Issues* 12: 799–827.

Lopez, Enrique. 1979. *The Harvard Mystique: The Power Syndrome That Affects Our Lives, from Sesame Street to the White House.* New York: Macmillan.

Lorenzo, Albert, and Krnacik, John. January 1986. "The Benchmark Poll." Public Opinion Survey. Marion, Mich.: Macomb Community College.

Louis Harris and Associates. 1975. *Public Opinion Survey: Public Perception of Leader Capacity to Know What People Want.* New York: Author.

―――. 1978. *Public Opinion Survey: Confidence in Leaders of Social Institutions.* New York: Author.

―――. 1980. *Public Opinion Survey: Confidence in Leaders of Social Institutions.* New York: Author.

―――. 1984. *Public Opinion Survey: Confidence in Leaders of Social Institutions.* New York: Author.

McKennell, A.C. 1978. "Cognition and Affect in Perceptions of Well-Being." *Social Indicators Research* 5: 389–426.

McLeod, Norman. 1984. "A Medley of Radio Winners." *CASE Currents* 10(3): 19.

March, James. 1982. "Developments in the Study of Organizations." *Review of Higher Education* 6: 1–17.

Mathews, David. October 1976. "Toward a New Purpose." *Change* 6: 62–63.

Media General Broadcast Services Survey. 1987. "College More Important Than Ever." *AGB Notes* 18(6).

Mitchell, Leon. 1983. "Tylenol Fights Back." *Public Relations Journal* 39(3): 10–14.

Mitroff, Ian. 2 March 1986. "Corporate Disaster Planning." *San Jose Mercury News.*

Moore, Beadle, et al. 1979. *Arkansas Attitudes on Higher Education: Results of a Survey of Arkansas Citizens.* Fayetteville: University of Arkansas, Center for Urban and Governmental Affairs. ED 176 709. 35 pp. MF–$1.07; PC–$5.79.

Morrell, Louis. May/June 1987. "Get Ready for Tomorrow's Crisis." *AGB Reports*: 44–46.

Mortimer, Kenneth, and McConnell, T. R. 1982. *Sharing Authority Effectively.* San Francisco: Jossey-Bass.

Mortimer, Kenneth P., and Tierney, Michael. 1979. *The Three R's of the Eighties: Reduction, Reallocation, and Retrenchment.* AAHE-ERIC Higher Education Report No. 4. Washington, D.C.: American Association for Higher Education. ED 172 642. 93 pp. MF–$1.07; PC–$10.03.

Myers, Judith. 1985. "Perfect Pitch." *CASE Currents* 11(4): 26–28.

Nettles, Michael. 1987. *The Emergence of College Outcome Assessment: Prospects for Enhancing State Colleges and Universities.* Working Paper. Princeton: New Jersey State College Governing Boards Association.

Nulty, Peter. 1985. "Arco Is No Sitting Duck." *Fortune* 112(13): 86–87.

Ohio Board of Regents. December 1987. *Guidelines for Program Excellence.* Columbus: Ohio Board of Regents.

Owings, Thomas. 1977. *Perspectives on Postsecondary Education: Alabama Citizens Survey 1977.* Tuscaloosa: University of Alabama, Institute of Higher Education Research and Services.

Parsons, Talcott, and Platt, G. 1972. *The American University.* New York: Free Press.

Patouillet, Leland. 1986. "Our Good-will Ambassadors." *CASE Currents* 12(1): 41–72.

Pauly, David, et al. 10 March 1986. *Newsweek*: 52–53.

Pelletier, S. G., and McNamara, W. 1985. "To Market?" *Educational Horizons* 63(2): 54–60.

Pendel, Mary. 1985. "Beyond Gallup." *CASE Currents* 11(7): 40–42.

Pfeffer, Jeffrey, and Salancik, Gerald. 1978. *The External Control of Organizations.* New York: Harper & Row.

Powell, William. 3 March 1986. "The Tylenol Rescue." *Newsweek*: 52–53.

Raley, Nancy. 1984. "A Medley of Radio Winners." *CASE Currents* 10(3): 18–23.

Rhodes, Lucien. 1982. "Sole Success." *Inc.* 4(2): 44–50.

Rokeach, Milton. 1968. *Beliefs, Attitudes, and Values.* San Francisco: Jossey-Bass.

Rossman, Jack. January 1975. *Attitudes toward Macalester's Program to Expand Educational Opportunities.* St. Paul. Minn.: Macalester College, Office of Institutional Research and Planning. ED 130 592. 24 pp. MF–$1.07; PC–$3.85.

Rubins, Debra. 1985. "Come on Up and See Us Sometime." *CASE Currents* 11(4): 18–20.

Saporito, William. 1983. "Kroger, The New King of Supermarketing." *Fortune* 107(4): 75–80.

Sasseen, Jane. 23 December 1985. "Sam Heyman's Hopeful Script for Carbide." *Business Week*: 30–31.

Scitovsky, T. 1976. *The Joyless Economy.* New York: Oxford University Press.

Selznick, Philip. 1949. *TVA and the Grass Roots: A Study in the Sociology of Formal Organization.* Berkeley: University of California Press.

Shell, Roberta. 1982. "Putting a Business Back Together Again." *Inc.* 4(3): 95–99.

Smith, Virginia. 1983. "What the Public Thinks: CASE-Inspired Survey Shows Strong Support of Higher Education." *CASE Currents* 9(1): 10–15.

Spitzberg, Irving. 1980. "Monitoring Social and Political Changes." In *Improving Academic Management: A Handbook of Planning and Institutional Research*, edited by Paul Jedamus and Marvin Peterson. San Francisco: Jossey-Bass.

Spooner, Lisa. October 1985. "Media and Marketing Tools Build a Strong Business Image." *Savings Institutions*: 86–90.

Stancill, James. January/February 1984. "Upgrade Your Company's Image and Valuation." *Harvard Business Review* 1: 16–20.

Stober, Arthur. 1984. "A Medley of Radio Winners." *CASE Currents* 10(3): 20.

Strenski, James. 1984. "Public Relations Challenges." *Public Relations Journal* 40(11): 41–42.

Thomas, P.S. 1980. "Environmental Scanning: The State of the Art." *Long Range Planning* 13: 20–25.

Topor, Robert S. 1985. "Going to the Market." *CASE Currents* 11(3): 25–26.

————. 1986. *Institutional Image: How to Define, Improve, Market It.* Washington, D.C.: Council for Advancement and Support of Education. ED 270 000. 80 pp. MF–$1.07; PC not available EDRS.

Trachtenburg, Stephen. 1984. "Let's Not Be Shy about Marketing." *AGB Reports* 26(6): 37–39.

Trent, James W., and Medsker, Leland L. 1968. *Beyond High School: A Psychological Study of 10,000 High School Graduates.* San Francisco: Jossey-Bass.

Troxler, William, and Jarrell, Judith. 1984. "Capital Ideas." *CASE Currents* 10(3): 46–48.

Turner, Toni, et al. 1984. "Whose Move Is It?" *CASE Currents* 10(4): 20–24.

U.S. Department of Health, Education, and Welfare. 1969. *Toward a Social Report.* Washington, D.C.: U.S. Government Printing Office.

Walster, E.; Walster, G.W.; and Berscheid, E. 1978. *Equality: Theory and Research.* Boston: Allyn & Bacon.

Walters, G., and Paul, G. 1970. *Consumer Behavior: An Integrated Framework.* Homewood, Ill.: Richard D. Irwin, Inc.

Wasem G. 1978. "Marketing for Profits and Nonprofits." In *Marketing in Nonprofit Organizations,* edited by P.J. Montana. New York: AMACOM.

Weaver, Barbara; Stevenson, Deborah; and Thompson, Jay, Jr. 1986. "From Practice to Policy: Influence of Ball State's University College on Institutional and State Policies."

Weick, Karl. 1978. "Educational Organizations as Loosely Coupled Systems." *Administrative Science Quarterly* 23: 541–52.

Weissman, Julie. 1987. "Marketing and Higher Education."
Unpublished comprehensive qualifying exam, The University of
Michigan.

Yankelovich, Daniel. 1987. "Bridging the Gap." *CASE Currents*
13(9): 24–27.

Zald, Meyer, and Denton, Patricia. 1963. "From Evangelism to
General Service: On the Transformation of Character of the
YMCA." *Administrative Science Quarterly* 8(2): 214–34.

Additional Readings

Anthony, Robert, and Herzlinger, Regina. 1980. *Management Control
in Nonprofit Organizations*. Homewood, Ill.: Richard D. Irwin, Inc.

Banaszewski, John. 1981. "Thirteen Ways to Get a Company in
Trouble." *Inc.* 3(8): 97–99.

Barton, David, ed. 1978. *Marketing Higher Education.* New
Directions for Higher Education No. 21. San Francisco: Jossey-
Bass.

Bernays, E.L. November 1947. "A Better Deal for Nurses."
American Journal of Nursing 47: 720–22.

Bloch, Peter. 1984. "The Wellness Movement: Imperatives for Health
Care Marketers." *Journal of Health Care Marketing* 4(1): 9–16.

Brooker, George, and Noble, Michael. 1984. "The Marketing of
Higher Education." *College and University* 60(3): 191–200.

Calvin, Geoffrey. 1983. "Lessons from a Hot Dog Maker's Ordeal."
Fortune 107(5): 77–82.

Carey, Carol. 1982. "A New Image for an Old Product." *Inc.* 4(6):
93–94.

Carlson, Robert O. 1968. "Public Relations." In *International
Encyclopedia of the Social Sciences*. New York: Macmillan.

Cunningham, Robert M., Jr. 16 April 1978. "Of Snake Oil and
. Science." *Hospitals* 52: 79–82.

———. 1 September 1982. "Hospital Marketing." *Hospitals*: 84–86.

Donnely, James, and George, William. 1981. *Marketing of Services.*
Chicago: American Marketing Association.

Dunkin, Amy. 18 November 1985. "How Department Stores Plan to
Get the Registers Ringing Again." *Business Week*: 66–67.

Engardio, Pete. 9 December 1985. "Eastern: Oh What a Difference a
Month Makes." *Business Week*: 42–43.

Evans, Dale; Fitzpatrick, Therese; and Howard-Ruben, Josie. January
1983. "A District." *American Journal of Nursing*: 52.

Falberg, Warren C., and Bonnem, Shirley. 1 June 1977. "Good
Marketing Helps Hospital Grow." *Hospitals* 51: 70–72.

Festinger, L. 1962. *A Theory of Cognitive Dissonance.* Stanford:
Stanford University Press.

Firoz, Mohammed Nadeem. 1982. "Marketing in Nonprofit Higher Education." Doctoral dissertation, North Texas State University.

Franz, Julie L. August 1982. "PR, Marketing Departments Linked in Hospitals' Drive to Fill Market Void." *Modern Healthcare*: 82–84.

Galvagni, William. 1 April 1981. "Hospitals Diversify to Thrive in a Competitive Environment." *Hospitals*: 131–36.

Grabowski, Stanley. 1981. *Marketing Higher Education*. AAHE-ERIC Higher Education Report No. 5. Washington D.C.: American Association for Higher Education. ED 214 445. 47 pp. MF–$1.07; PC–$5.79.

Greenberg, Ellen. Winter 1982. "Competing for Scarce Resources." *Journal of Business Strategy*: 81–87.

Hafer, John, and Joiner, Carl. "Nurses as Image Emissaries: Are Role Conflicts Impinging on a Potential Asset for an Internal Marketing Strategy?" *Journal of Health Care Marketing* 4(1).

Hamner, James E., and Sax-Jacobs, Barbara J. "The Media, Communication, and Health Policy." University of Tennessee Center for the Health Sciences.

Harrell, Gilbert. *Consumer Behavior*. Orlando, Fla.: Harcourt Brace Jovanovich.

Hauser, Les J. 1 September 1984. "10 Reasons Hospital Marketing Programs Fail." *Hospitals*: 74.

Hillestad, Steven, and Berkowitz, Eric N. January 1982. "Hospital Executives Need Marketing Tools to Meet Competition Challenges." *Modern Healthcare:* 84–86.

Hunt, Shelby D. July 1976. "The Nature and Scope of Marketing." *Journal of Marketing* 40: 17–28.

Ialenti, Vincent S., and Lauroesch, William. 1985. "Community College Faculty Attitudes toward Their Role in Image-Building Activities." *Community/Junior College Quarterly of Research and Practice* 9(2): 119–28.

Ireland, Richard C. 1 June 1977. "Using Marketing Strategies to Put Hospitals on Target." *Hospitals* 51: 54–58.

Jackson, Thomas J. 1985. "Bolstering Graduate School Enrollments through Effective Use of Marketing." *College and University* 60 (3): 210–18.

Kalisch, Philip, and Kalisch, Beatrice. April 1982a. "The Image of the Nurse in Motion Pictures." *American Journal of Nursing*: 605–11.

———. April 1982b. "The Image of Nurses in Novels." *American Journal of Nursing*: 1120–24.

Kaplan, Michael D. 16 September 1979. "What It Is, What It Isn't." *Hospitals*: 176ff.

Karr, David. 1 June 1977. "Increasing a Hospital's Market Share." *Hospitals* 51: 64–66.

Kinkead, Gwen. 1984. "The Still Amazing Cigarette Game." *Fortune* 110(5): 70–72.

Kotler, Philip. April 1972. "A Generic Concept of Marketing." *Journal of Marketing* 36: 46–54.

———. 1975. *Marketing for Nonprofit Organizations*. Englewood Cliffs, N.J.: Prentice-Hall.

———. January 1979. "Strategies for Introducing Marketing into Nonprofit Organizations." *Journal of Marketing* 43: 37–44.

———. 1983. *Principles of Marketing*. 2d ed. Englewood Cliffs, N.J.: Prentice-Hall.

Kotler, Philip, and Levy, Sidney. January 1969a. "Broadening the Concept of Marketing." *Journal of Marketing* 33: 10–15.

———. January 1969b. "A New Form of Marketing Myopia: Rejoinder to Professor Luck." *Journal of Marketing* 33: 55–57.

Krachenberg, A.R. May 1972. "Bringing the Concept of Marketing to Higher Education." *Journal of Higher Education* 43: 369–80.

Levitt, Theodore. 1969. *The Marketing Mode: Pathways to Corporate Growth*. New York: McGraw-Hill.

Lindeman, Carol. 1932. "Images and Audience." In *Image-Making in Nursing*. American Academy of Nursing.

Litten, Larry, et al. 1983. *Applying Market Research in College Admissions*. New York: College Entrance Exam Board. ED 238 341. 324 pp. MF–$1.07; PC–$28.76.

Lovelock, Christopher H. Fall 1977. "Concepts and Strategies for Health Marketers." *Hospital and Health Services Administration:* 75–79.

———. 1984a. *Marketing for Public and Nonprofit Managers*. New York: John Wiley & Sons.

———. 1984b. *Services Marketing*. Englewood Cliffs, N.J.: Prentice-Hall.

Lovelock, Christopher, and Weinberg, Charles. 1978. *Readings in Public and Nonprofit Marketing*. Scientific Press.

Lucas, John, ed. 1979. *Developing a Total Marketing Plan*. New Directions for Institutional Research No. 21. San Francisco: Jossey-Bass.

Luck, David J. July 1969. "Broadening the Concept of Marketing— Too Far." *Journal of Marketing* 33: 53–55.

McMillan, Norman H. 16 November, 1981. "Marketing: A Tool That Serves Hospitals' Survival Instincts." *Hospitals*: 89–92.

Mangione, Thomas. "The Image of a University: The University of Massachusetts–Boston." Survey Research Program. University of Massachusetts–Boston, Office of Educational Planning.

Marshall, John F., and Delman, Jeffrey M. 1985. "Researching Institutional Image: The Development and Implementation of a Market Research Plan for Educational Institutions." *College and University* 59(4): 316–33.

Meyerowitz, Steven. 1985. "Bankruptcy: The Strategic Wild Card." *Business Marketing* 70(11): 88–92.

Petre, Peter. 3 September 1984. "Searle's Big Pitch for a Tiny Ingredient." *Fortune*: 73.

Rados, David. 1982. *Marketing for Nonprofit Organizations*. 2d ed. Englewood Cliffs, N.J.: Prentice-Hall.

Rice, James A.; Slack, Richard S.; and Garside, Pamela A. 16 November 1981. "Hospitals Can Learn Valuable Marketing Strategies from Hotels." *Hospitals:* 95–98.

Rothschild, Michael L. 1977. *An Incomplete Bibliography of Works Relating to Marketing for Public Sector and Nonprofit Organizations*. 2d ed. Boston: Intercollegiate Case Clearing House.

Rothschild, William. 1976. *Putting It All Together: A Guide to Strategic Thinking*. New York: AMACOM.

Selby, Cecily Cannan. September/October 1978. "Better Performance from 'Nonprofits'." *Harvard Business Review*: 92–98.

Shapiro, Benson P. September/October 1973. "Marketing for Nonprofit Organizations." *Harvard Business Review*: 123–32.

Sherman, Stratford P. 1983. "Eastern Airlines on the Brink." *Fortune* 108(3): 102–12.

Shostack, Lynn. April 1977. "Breaking Free from Product Marketing." *Journal of Marketing*: 73–80.

Silber, John. 1980. Marketing Higher Education: The Survival Value of Integrity." *The National Journal of the ACAD* 24(3): 6.

Stiff, Ronald. Fall 1982. "The Nonprofit/Service Organization as a Marketing Research Problem: Issues and Examples." *Journal of Marketing Education:* 43–46.

Struckman-Johnson, Cindy, and Kinsley, Steven. 1985. "Assessment and Comparison of College Image among High School Seniors, College Students, and Alumni." *College and University* 60(4): 316–27.

Stuehler, George, Jr. 1 May 1980. "How Hospitals' Marketing and Planning Relate." *Hospitals*: 96–99.

Tracy, Johnson. 1984. "Toxic Shocker." *Fortune* 110(2): 48.

Walters, James C. 1984. "Breaking Down the Secrets of Market Research: An Essay Review." *College and University* 59(4): 378–81.

Witt, John A., and McRoberts, Nelson L. April 1983. "Marketing and Competition: Lack of Expertise, Funding Shackles Marketing Moves." *Modern Healthcare*: 75–78.

Zaltman, Gerald, and Bonoma, Thomas, eds. 1978. *Review of Marketing 1978*. American Marketing Association.

INDEX

A

AT&T, 47

Accountability
    campus unrest, 16
    constituent involvement, 66
    curricular reforms, 18, 22
    demands, 2, 13
    state assessment incentives, 73, 82
    two-year college demands, 15
    undergraduate performance, 34

ACT/COMP test, 75

Administrators
    executive development, 43
    goals/values, 33, 62
    role in image management, 107

Admissions selectivity, 10

Adult University (Cornell), 67

Advertising
    Army, 52-53
    campus outreach, 69-70
    labor unions, 54
    regaining consumer confidence, 42
    state/local government issues, 53

Affect: element of stature, 10, 30, 114

AIDS: crisis potential, 111

Alaska oil pipeline impact, 46

Allstate Insurance, 53

Alumni
    accomplishments, 10
    educational programs, 67
    interest surveys, 65
    lobbying, 71
    outreach volunteers, 70

Alumni Association Legislative Network, 71

Alverno College, 72

American Institute of Certified Public Accountants, 72

American Medical Association, 51

American University, 70

Appalachia, 11

Army advertising, 52-53

Assessment
    Alverno College, 72
    comprehensive, 102-103
    enhancing quality, 61
    Northeast Missouri State University, 71-72

outcomes, 81-82, 83, 101-106
published data, 71
state incentives, 73-74, 82
strategic, 79-80, 83
University of Tennessee at Knoxville, 72-73
value-added program, 71
Athletic scandal, 76-77
Atlantic Richfield Corporation, 46
Attitude: as component of stature, 6-7

B
Ball State University, 73-74
Basic skills
assessment, 102
standards, 74
"Be All You Can Be" campaign, 53
Bell System, 40
Bendix Corporation, 45
Benefits of education, 5, 22, 66
Bennett, William J., 1
Berea College, 11
Bhopal, India disaster, 44, 46, 110
Boeing Co., 47
Bok, Derek, 14
Business/industry
collaboration with academe, 64
consumer confidence, 41-42
corporate style, 43
crisis management, 44-45
deregulation effects, 40
distinctiveness, 45
enhancing stature, 40-47
innovation capacity, 43
product visibility, 42
social responsibility, 46
strategic decisions, 45
talent capacity, 43
Business Week, 40

C
California Legislator to Campus Program, 68
Campus unrest, 16, 17
Carnegie-Mellon University, 11
Carter, Jimmy, 17, 20

---

value of education, 25
Gerber baby food tampering, 44
Goals
    academic outcomes, 80-81
    achievement vs. public perception, 61-62
    administrators, 33
    assessment, 102
    faculty, 32, 33
    higher education, 5, 62
    institutional, 37, 76, 80
    media techniques, 70
    statewide, 65
Government agencies
    Army advertising, 52-53
    collaboration with academe, 64
    legislator campus involvement, 67
    public credibility, 18, 53-54
    state/local image, 53
Governing boards, 76
Grading options, 18
Graduate Record Examinations (GRE), 72, 73
Graduate surveys, 81
Grants, 10
GRE (see Graduate Record Examinations)
Greater Tampa Chamber of Commerce, 70
Group Attitudes Corporation, 25

H
Harris surveys: public confidence, 16, 18, 21, 23
Harvard Business Review, 40
Harvard University, 11, 114
Health care organizations
    competition, 48-49
    marketing/public relations, 47-48
    stature enhancement techniques, 48
High school/college relationships, 109-110
Higher education
    collaborative efforts, 64
    enhancing stature, 78, 83, 86
    goals: early 1960s, 5
    image management, 106-111
    lack of confidence in, 16
    outreach programs, 68-71
    performance attributes, 33-36
    practices to adopt, 78-84
    principles for (table), 55-58

International Harvester, 42
"Interview Possibility" radio guides, 69

J
Johnson & Johnson, 44

K
Kent State University, 17
Kroger Company, 44

L
Labor unions, 54
Leader Federal Bank, 42
Leadership
    academic, 75-78
    decline in public confidence, 18-20, 21
    element of stature, 10
    government officials, 53-54
    public perception (figures), 19, 22, 25
    relationship to organization, 76
Legal advice, 46
Legislatures (see also Lobbying)
    campus support, 73
    visitation programs, 67-68
Leveraging strategies
    image management, 106-111
    outcomes assessment, 101-106
    resource allocation, 98-101
    strategic assessment, 90-97
Library size, 10
Licensure examinations, 72, 73
Lobbying, 70, 71
Logos, 41, 63

M
Management information systems, 79, 97
Market research
    Army, 53
    crisis management, 41-42
Marketing
    cost clarification, 105
    current literature on, 2
    difference from stature, 7
    distinctiveness, 47
    enrollment stabilization, 31

new image creation, 42
public opinion, 22
short-term strategies, 62
student recruitment, 20
Martin Marietta Corporation, 45
Massachusetts Institute of Technology, 11
Master plans, 65
McNeil Corporation, 41-42, 44
Media coverage
campus outreach, 69-70
college visibility, 64
nursing "media watch," 50-51
physicians, 51-52
scandal, 46
Medicine: stature enhancement, 51-52
Merck, 47
Military
public confidence in, 18, 21
stature enhancement, 53
Mills College, 64
Mission statements, 34
Model of stature, 8-9, 12, 85
Montana State University, 70
Morehouse College, 11
Myers-Briggs Type Indicator, 75

N

Name change, 42
National Broadcasting Corporation, 42
National Collegiate Athletic Association, 77
National Opinion Research Center, 18, 21
National Steel, 44
National surveys: public opinion, 15
National Teacher Examinations (NTE), 72
Navistar, 42
New York City: economics, 17
New York State Education Department, 66
New York Times, 46
Newsline, 69
Newspapers, 64
Nixon, Richard, 16, 17
Northeast Missouri State University, 71-72
Northeastern University Radio Network, 69
Not-for-profit organizations
government agencies, 52-54
labor unions, 54

Rubbermaid, 43

S

San Diego State University, 66
SAT (see Scholastic Aptitude Test)
Satisfaction
       element of stature, 10, 114
       outcomes measure, 104-105
       societal condition influence, 30
       student, 104-105
Scandal, 46, 76-77
"Scanning team," 91
Scholastic Aptitude Test (SAT), 15, 77
Search committees, 76-77
Selectivity, 10
Sierra Club, 46
Smith College, 11
Social institutions
       confidence in, 18-20, 21
       leaders (figures), 22, 224
Social responsibility, 46
Societal conditions
       changes, 2, 5, 29
       component of stature systems model, 30
       influence on public opinion, 13-15
       monitoring, 104
       overview 1965-1970, 15-16
       overview 1971-1975, 17-18
       overview 1976-1980, 20-21
       overview 1981-1985, 23
South Florida University, 70
Southern Methodist University, 76-77
Sputnik, 5
State action
       academic standards, 74
       assessment programs, 73-75
       financial incentives, 72, 82
       statewide planning, 65-66
State legislators, 67-68, 71
Stature
       activity domains/practices for academe (table), 87-90
       axes determining variation (figure), 11
       definition, 6-8
       dimensions of, 8-12, 29, 61
       enhancement practices, 39-40, 48

ASHE-ERIC HIGHER EDUCATION REPORTS

Since 1983, the Association for the Study of Higher Education (ASHE) and the ERIC Clearinghouse on Higher Education at the George Washington University have cosponsored the ASHE-ERIC Higher Education Report series. The 1987 series is the sixteenth overall, with the American Association for Higher Education having served as cosponsor before 1983.

Each monograph is the definitive analysis of a tough higher education problem, based on thorough research of pertinent literature and institutional experiences. After topics are identified by a national survey, noted practitioners and scholars write the reports, with experts reviewing each manuscript before publication.

Eight monographs (10 monographs before 1985) in the ASHE-ERIC Higher Education Report series are published each year, available individually or by subscription. Subscription to eight issues is $60 regular; $50 for members of AERA, AAHE, and AIR; $40 for members of ASHE (add $7.50 for postage outside the United States).

Prices for single copies, including 4th class postage and handling, are $10.00 regular and $7.50 for members of AERA, AAHE, AIR, and ASHE ($7.50 regular and $6.00 for members for 1983 and 1984 reports, $6.50 regular and $5.00 for members for reports published before 1983). If faster 1st class postage is desired for U.S. and Canadian orders, add $.75 for each publication ordered; overseas, add $4.50. For VISA and MasterCard payments, include card number, expiration date, and signature. Orders under $25 must be prepaid. Bulk discounts are available on orders of 15 or more reports (not applicable to subscriptions). Order from the Publications Department, ASHE-ERIC Higher Education Reports, the George Washington University, One Dupont Circle, Suite 630, Washington, D.C. 20036-1183, or phone us at 202/296-2597. Write for a publication list of all the Higher Education Reports available.

1987 ASHE-ERIC Higher Education Reports

1. Incentive Early Retirement Programs for Faculty: Innovative Responses to a Changing Environment
   Jay L. Chronister and Thomas R. Kepple, Jr.

2. Working Effectively with Trustees: Building Cooperative Campus Leadership
   Barbara E. Taylor

3. Formal Recognition of Employer-Sponsored Instruction: Conflict and Collegiality in Postsecondary Education
   Nancy S. Nash and Elizabeth M. Hawthorne

4. Learning Styles: Implications for Improving Educational Practices
   Charles S. Claxton and Patricia H. Murrell

5. Higher Education Leadership: Enhancing Skills through Professional Development Programs
   Sharon A. McDade

6. Higher Education and the Public Trust: Improving Stature in Colleges and Universities
   Richard L. Alfred and Julie Weissman

1986 ASHE-ERIC Higher Education Reports

1. Post-tenure Faculty Evaluation: Threat or Opportunity?
   Christine M. Licata

2. Blue Ribbon Commissions and Higher Education: Changing Academe from the Outside
   Janet R. Johnson and Lawrence R. Marcus

3. Responsive Professional Education: Balancing Outcomes and Opportunities
   Joan S. Stark, Malcolm A. Lowther, and Bonnie M.K. Hagerty

4. Increasing Students' Learning: A Faculty Guide to Reducing Stress among Students
   Neal A. Whitman, David C. Spendlove, and Claire H. Clark

5. Student Financial Aid and Women: Equity Dilemma?
   Mary Moran

6. The Master's Degree: Tradition, Diversity, Innovation
   Judith S. Glazer

7. The College, the Constitution, and the Consumer Student: Implications for Policy and Practice
   Robert M. Hendrickson and Annette Gibbs

8. Selecting College and University Personnel: The Quest and the Questions
   Richard A. Kaplowitz

1985 ASHE-ERIC Higher Education Reports

1. Flexibility in Academic Staffing: Effective Policies and Practices
   Kenneth P. Mortimer, Marque Bagshaw, and Andrew T. Masland

2. Associations in Action: The Washington, D.C., Higher Education Community
   Harland G. Bloland

3. And on the Seventh Day: Faculty Consulting and Supplemental Income
   Carol M. Boyer and Darrell R. Lewis

4. Faculty Research Performance: Lessons from the Sciences and Social Sciences
   John W. Creswell

5. Academic Program Reviews: Institutional Approaches, Expectations, and Controversies
   Clifton F. Conrad and Richard F. Wilson

6. Students in Urban Settings: Achieving the Baccalaureate Degree
   Richard C. Richardson, Jr., and Louis W. Bender

7. Serving More Than Students: A Critical Need for College Student Personnel Services
   Peter H. Garland

8. Faculty Participation in Decision Making: Necessity or Luxury?
   Carol E. Floyd

1984 ASHE-ERIC Higher Education Reports

1. Adult Learning: State Policies and Institutional Practices
   K. Patricia Cross and Anne-Marie McCartan

2. Student Stress: Effects and Solutions
   Neal A. Whitman, David C. Spendlove, and Claire H. Clark

3. Part-time Faculty: Higher Education at a Crossroads
   Judith M. Gappa

4. Sex Discrimination Law in Higher Education: The Lessons of the Past Decade
   J. Ralph Lindgren, Patti T. Ota, Perry A. Zirkel, and Nan Van Gieson

5. Faculty Freedoms and Institutional Accountability: Interactions and Conflicts
   Steven G. Olswang and Barbara A. Lee

6. The High-Technology Connection: Academic/Industrial Cooperation for Economic Growth
   Lynn G. Johnson

7. Employee Educational Programs: Implications for Industry and Higher Education
   Suzanne W. Morse

8. Academic Libraries: The Changing Knowledge Centers of Colleges and Universities
   Barbara B. Moran

9. Futures Research and the Strategic Planning Process: Implications for Higher Education
   James L. Morrison, William L. Renfro, and Wayne I. Boucher

10. Faculty Workload: Research, Theory, and Interpretation
    Harold E. Yuker

1983 ASHE-ERIC Higher Education Reports

1. The Path to Excellence: Quality Assurance in Higher Education
   Laurence R. Marcus, Anita O. Leone, and Edward D. Goldberg

2. Faculty Recruitment, Retention, and Fair Employment: Obligations and Opportunities
   John S. Waggaman

3. Meeting the Challenges: Developing Faculty Careers*
   Michael C.T. Brookes and Katherine L. German

4. Raising Academic Standards: A Guide to Learning Improvement
   Ruth Talbott Keimig

5. Serving Learners at a Distance: A Guide to Program Practices
   Charles E. Feasley

6. Competence, Admissions, and Articulation: Returning to the Basics in Higher Education
   Jean L. Preer

7. Public Service in Higher Education: Practices and Priorities
   Patricia H. Crosson

8. Academic Employment and Retrenchment: Judicial Review and Administrative Action
   Robert M. Hendrickson and Barbara A. Lee

9. Burnout: The New Academic Disease*
   Winifred Albizu Meléndez and Rafael M. de Guzmán

10. Academic Workplace: New Demands, Heightened Tensions
    Ann E. Austin and Zelda F. Gamson

*Out-of-print. Available through EDRS.

Dear Educator,

I welcome the ASHE-ERIC monograph series. The series is a service to those who need brief but dependable analyses of key issues in higher education.
    (Rev.) Theodore M. Hesburgh, C.S.C.
    President Emeritus, University of Notre Dame

Order Form

Quantity   Amount

_____ Please enter my subscription to the 1987 ASHE-ERIC
Higher Education Reports at $60.00, 25% off the cover
price.   _____

_____ Please enter my subscription to the 1988 Higher Edu- _____
cation Reports at $60.00.

_____ Outside U.S., add $7.50 for postage per series.   _____

Individual reports are available at the following prices:
1985 and forward, $10.00 each.
1983 and 1984, $7.50 each.
1982 and back, $6.50 each.

Please send me the following reports:

_____ Report No. ____ (_____)   _____
_____ Report No. ____ (_____)   _____
_____ Report No. ____ (_____)   _____
                                              SUBTOTAL: _____
            Optional U.P.S. Shipping ($1.00 per book) _____
                          TOTAL AMOUNT DUE: _____

NOTE: All prices subject to change.

Name _____

Title _____

Institution _____

Address _____

_____

City _____ State _____ ZIP _____

Phone _____

Signature _____
☐ Check enclosed, payable to ASHE.   ☐ Purchase order attached.
☐ Please charge my credit card:
              ☐ VISA   ☐ MasterCard (check one)

Expiration date _____

Send to: ASHE-ERIC Higher Education Reports
The George Washington University
One Dupont Circle, Suite 630, Dept. G4
Washington, D.C. 20036-1183

NOTES

NOTES

NOTES

NOTES

NOTES

NOTES